neopolitics

**what makes
modern politics
so different?**

Igor Lys © 2019
ISBN: 9781798088036
Cover: author's design
Translated from French
Corrections & proofreading in French: Lisa Scalco, Michael Brunet
Published by GAMBIT
gambit-delys.com

igor lys

This is not a book on political communication. Nor is it a manual of manipulation, storytelling, media combat. After having read it, you will not be able to automatically win every election and dominate every TV debate. Communication consultant, you will not have any magic keys to sell to your client for the price of a small house; young elected official, you will not be able to build an incredible career to become, in a few years, the President of Humanity.

This is not a magical book that makes empty promises; it is, actually, quite the opposite. A book that will help you not to be like all those who, according to more or less eccentric theories and more or less cynical techniques, promise you things. "Just buy this book, and you'll become a millionaire" - or, "Just vote for this candidate, and you'll find happiness". This book is intended to be a remedy against false promises. It teaches how not to use them, and how to stay a winner still. How, as a politician, you can, using specific techniques, remain attractive to the electorate, strong in negotiation, effective in the implementation of decisions - and honest. No magic, no promise except to offer you a reflection on the current state of the world and on the tools that allow you to improve. All while ensuring many victories against opponents who do not hesitate to strike low blows in the everlasting battle for power.

Of course, if you are not a man or woman working in politics, this book may still be useful to you. The solutions proposed in it are, in a way, universal, and the overview of the social phenomena can be instructive regardless of your field of expertise. For example, the vision of the "personal brand map" described in this book can help you build stronger relationships with your family, your colleagues - and better resist your opponents, for example in your company.

Enjoy the reading!

neopolitics

table of contents

Introduction 6

    The wounds of politics 13

    Politics is dead, long live neopolitics 28

    Data in politics 37

        Data as political capital 43

        Data as political intelligence 45

        Data as political influence 48

        And it works? 50

    Intermediate Bodies and Participative Democracy in Neopolitics 55

    The Neotruth 78

Part 2. Neopolitical marketing 94

    Political brands 99

    The Neopolitical Brand Matrix 108

    Permanent competition and the media 24 hours a day 130

Conclusion 144

igor lys

neopolitics

Introduction

It is Saturday, December 15, 2018. I cross the Avenue de la Grande Armée in Paris. To my righthand side, a wall of policemen. To my left, hundreds of people, scattered on the road, united by a detail of clothing: they all wear a yellow vest. Symbol of an unprecedented since decades social protest in France, they occupy the headlines of all newspapers, shake up the political and civil agenda, and send shock waves to as far as Russia or the United States. Vladimir Putin and Donald Trump comment on them. The far-right German party, AfD, is trying to seize the symbol and is organizing "yellow" protests in Berlin. The world is stunned by the impressive images of the tagged Arc de Triomphe. If we listen to journalists, politicians and experts, everyone knew that this wave of protest would emerge, but everyone remained deaf to the grumbling of deep France.

At the end of 2018, France was indeed only interested in yellow vests, but the whole world was not short of burning political issues (and that is a first-class euphemism). In Washington, Donald Trump is preparing for what will be one of the strangest (and the longest) shutdowns in the country's history. Britain is about a month away from refusing the Brexit agreement, and Brazil is waiting for President Bolsonaro to take office, not knowing yet that he will start his presidency with the most ridiculous decisions (and by posing with a gun in front of the cameras). Yemen remains the world's worst humanitarian disaster, the Crown Prince of Saudi Arabia is not accountable for the crime the CIA says he committed, and in snowy Moscow, Vladimir Putin is pleased with what the world will learn a few weeks later: the withdrawal of American troops from Syria.

So many things that many observers describe as unexpected, or even incredible. The reliability of big data in politics seemed infallible, technocratic models of governance were, according to an increasing number of specialists, the only answer to the challenges of the time. From the Berlin Chancellery in Merkel to the dark cabinets of Staraya Square in Moscow, housing Putin's almighty Administration, from the Chinese Communist Party HQ to the meeting rooms in Kenya, almost everyone agreed on one thing: the politics was predictable and controllable.

neopolitics

And then, the harsh return to reality. As Patrick Artus, Chief Economist of Natixis, said so well at a conference in Paris in January 2019, "we economists are perfectly rational beings, which is why we are so often wrong". The world is not done surprising us.

Young President Macron discovers the reality of managing a country. The diabolical *Cambridge Analytica* must deal with public pressure for transparency and respect. Jim Mattis, an imperturbable soldier famous for his phrase "be polite, be professional, but have a plan to kill all everyone you meet", freaks out and leaves Trump's administration, and Trump in turn really only sends him away after reading the press' reactions to the general's letter of resignation. All this and many other examples raise the question: what is happening to politics today?

As you read this, new ways of governing, communicating, new hierarchies and new powers are emerging. And the old ones - those some of us still believe to be modern - are changing, as do their forms and structures.

Important changes in our societies have been brought, on the one hand, by social and geopolitical phenomena that current generations are not able to manage in their entirety (such as mass immigration, climate change, the evolution of theory and practices of war, etc.) and, on the other hand, by a completely new civil involvement made possible by a much-facilitated exchange of information. This new system, which imperceptibly replaces, element by element, what we still believe to be politics, transforms the way important decisions are made today and, above all, changes those who make them.

We still live with the old immutable structures: Parliaments, Presidents, ministers, departments and associations, and we continue to assign decision-making to them as has been the case for hundreds of years (although this is just as questionable). Members of Parliament are elected by universal suffrage, Presidents and Prime Ministers make decisions that governments implement. And in countries we call less democratic, authoritarian leaders use power mechanisms to control the entire political spectrum and hunt down the opposition...

But is that really the way it works? Knowing that private companies generate more money than many countries in the industrial world; that so many influences weigh on the electorate at so many levels that votes are no longer allocated to the voters themselves but to the sophisticated calculations of large agencies, the brokers of influence; that individuals outside the political sphere often have more power than those at the top of the electoral pyramid, etc. etc...

So what exactly are we talking about when we use the word "politics"?

From the Ubeid period in Mesopotamia to the great national debate in early 2019 in France, politics is at the heart of everything for a fairly simple reason: we are all, as humans, Aristotle's political animals. Even if we think we have pulled ourselves out of this type of governance, even if we live in a forest (or any kind of "outstated" place, like ZADs in France) cut off from any social link, we will be a part of politics at least because of the example we represent, the image we give and on which others build their discourses.

With a clearly negative connotation, the word "politics" comes back to poison the discussions, evoking this much-discussed "political politics". In lounges, bars, universities and factories around the world, politics is disgusting and fascinating. It is the scapegoat, the source of all evils and the answer to all questions, which millions of people identify as their enemy. Forgetting that one of the greatest fighters against the "system", Odoacre - the very one who deposed the last Roman emperor, Romulus Augustus, - did not hesitate long before taking the title of patrician of the same Rome of which he had ensured the fall.

Political science, as a discipline that seeks to explain and improve the, say, intellectual framework of governance, must respond to a whole range of new challenges - but for the most part composed of elements that have been known for centuries. But political practice, i.e. the set of tools used to acquire and exercise power, no longer has anything to do with the reality faced by the first readers of the *Prince* of Machiavelli. And this practice, which is reinvented every day in the face of new technological, societal and economic phenomena, is so far removed from political science, from politics strictly speaking, that I prefer to call it *neopolitics*. While political science will continue to rely on Hobbs and Rousseau, Locke and Plato, neopolitics will study big data, NLP and social dynamics in networks, personal branding and algorithms. In other words, it will study the practice of gouvernance and management in a connected, technologically "compressed" - and, more than ever, chaotic - world.

I am convinced, after 10 years of working in private diplomacy and managing political and cultural projects between the most diverse countries, that it is by creating a new toolbox based on the ever-changing socio-technological context that solutions for better governance will be designed. The need for these new tools exists both among political actors and among citizens, who are seeking - this is an objective reality confirmed by an impressive array of facts - to always better understand and participate in politics. On the one hand, to better define and communicate one's message, and on the other hand, to better decipher the signals and better build its citizen action.

This little book is a first step in the reflection on these tools, which are necessary for both actors and spectators of political life, whatever the country, culture and setting. To the actors, because it is important to be aware of the current context, to know how modern influences work so as not to be a mere victim of communication agencies and their turnkey solutions, often without much interest because they are excessively technical. To spectators, because decoding messages and categorizing political offers (and their carriers) makes it possible to transport the often emotional and irrational debate to the field of functional analysis, and therefore that of serious proposals and comments.

To come to these instruments, we will first talk - without overloading the reader with unnecessary depths, because he will surely be able to do his own research according to the proposed references - about these changes that shake up our habits. It is important to understand that, even if every generation, or almost every generation, since millennia believes that it is experiencing a dramatic change in governance, what we are experiencing today is unique, if only because of the unprecedented nature of the technological changes that accompany us.

Then, I will present the key elements of these changes, in particular the use of big data for political purposes, and the speed of media reaction that imposes a completely new dynamic on political action and radically changes its form. I will of course talk about the concrete solutions that exist as answers to these new challenges, so that the public, as well as specialists, are aware of recent trends.

Finally, to conclude, I will come back to what has been the basis of political marketing for decades, such as the personal brand, the program, political communication and the semantics of campaigns and the exercise of power. All these elements, some of which are defined by the ancient (*The Prince*) or very ancient (Sun Tzu's *Art of War*) works, are not fixed and are the first to change under the winds of History - which we all feel is blowing.

igor lys

The wounds of politics

In 1969, an American by the name of Karl Hess - a political philosopher, working hard for the Republican Party for which he was the author of the strategies in 1960 and 1964, one of the pioneers of the emerging neoliberal movement, as well as a motorcycle racing enthusiast - published an article in Playboy magazine. The immediate proximity of the naked female bodies does not detract from the intellectual quality of his writing, dedicated to the defence of the ultraliberal "laissez-faire society". His article is entitled *The Death of Politics*. The death of politics, no less! Here is what he says in his conclusion:

neopolitics

"Power and authority, as substitutes for performance and rational thought, are the specters that haunt the world today. They are the ghosts of awed and superstitious yesterdays. And politics is their familiar. Politics, throughout time, has been an institutionalized denial of man's ability to survive through the exclusive employment of all his own powers for his own welfare. And politics, throughout time, has existed solely through the resources that it has been able to plunder from the creative and productive people whom it has, in the name of many causes and moralities, denied the exclusive employment of all their own powers for their own welfare.

Ultimately, this must mean that politics denies the rational nature of man. Ultimately, it means that politics is just another form of residual magic in our culture — a belief that somehow things come from nothing; that things may be given to some without first taking them from others; that all the tools of man's survival are his by accident or divine right and not by pure and simple inventiveness and work"

In this text, where the American approach is so clearly obvious, and which could delight both John Stuart Mill and Ayn Rand (but especially the great theorist of libertarianism Robert Nozick - and Voltaire), Hess explains, brandishing the state as the most horrible of scarecrows, that politics is dead. In the context of the revolts, which were so much more violent than what the French knew with yellow vests (the "events" in Detroit in 1967 alone resulted in the destruction of more than 400 buildings, 7200 arrests, 467 wounded and 43 dead - in just 5 days), Hess' response was unambiguous: nothing was going well anymore. A fierce fighter against the welfare state if not the state in general ("for different purposes, [conservatives and liberals] see the state as an instrument not protecting man's freedom but either instructing or restricting how that freedom is to be used"), he comes to the following conclusion: politics, being an extension of power based on repression, has shown its limits, by allowing all this American social violence of the time to emerge. And, by showing its limits, it became a victim of itself. According to Hess, politics died in the 1960s, since it failed to protect people from state violence, but rather generated it. And so, as it was proposed in Playboy, we had to move on.

Hess, this representative of so-called classical liberalism, spoke of politics in the sense used by bistro regulars, with a direct negative connotation: it is for him the "familiar" of "power and authority" (themselves the "ghosts of the past"), a box containing dishonest practices aimed at limiting individual freedom. But what about politics in the academic sense? Hess did not talk about it (because for him, as for many Liberals, the intellectualization of politics was a way of giving it the legitimacy it did not deserve). But a few years earlier, in 1961, in a relatively small American journal *The Western Political Quarterly* published by Utah State University, a certain James Holton wrote in an article entitled *Is Political Philosophy Dead?*: "Political philosophy exists today as a mere shadow of itself". Why? Because, Holton explains, "the decline of political philosophy is part of the decline of rationality and ideas as such". The decline of rationality, in 2019 this is no stranger to us, with all the obscurantist protests spread on social networks. From anti-vaxxers to conspiracy theorists of all kinds, from Islamist groups to American Christian sects, as Pierre Bourdieu rightly said in 1999, "obscurantism has returned but this time we are dealing with people who pretend to come from the side of reason".

In the 1960s, in a context of systemic crisis, social and intellectual dynamics already predicted the societal earthquakes of the 1970s. Technological developments, combined with the fallout from the post-traumatic shock of the post-war period, unprecedented economic growth and the unprecedented dynamics of the Cold War that were calling for a great social and scientific progress, have led to a serious challenge to what David DeHaas calls[1] "human identity". The American revolts, the assassinations of John Kennedy and Martin Luther King, the May 1968 protests in France, the Iranian revolution of 1963, the 32 African independences, 17 of which took place in

---

[1] *The Crises of Human Identity in 1960*, in *The Appolon Digital Journal*, avril 2017

1960 alone, the flight of Commander Gagarin, the "true" birth of feminism and the end of political "warming" (*ottepel*) in the USSR - all this has so shaken up the reality of the peoples that it should not be surprising that the end of the decade seemed to many to be that of an era. Judiciously ridiculed by Jacques Derrida and knowingly corrected by Samuel Huntington, Francis Fukuyama announced to us, twenty years later, the end of History. The roots of this drama attitude may have to be found in the 1960s.

Today, we are in a way reliving the profound dynamics of those years. We cannot compare the two periods, even if the temptation is great, but we see a crucial similarity in understanding what this little book tries to demonstrate: scientific and technological progress creates *modi vivendi* and *modi operandi*, especially in the media sphere, that find no precedent in human history. While crises in the perception of politics are recurrent (the crisis of the "Thirty Tyrants" that Athens experienced in 404 would be very conceivable in 2404), new ways of accessing knowledge and other citizens make it increasingly difficult to predict the outcome of the crisis.

One of the key elements of the current period is the fact that the overwhelming majority of political actors find themselves - or rather, have found themselves - in the position of Bertrand Russell's "inductivist turkey". As a

neopolitics

reminder, here it is brilliantly presented by Alan Chalmers[2]:

> "As soon as it arrived at the turkey farm in the morning, a turkey noticed that it was being fed at 9 a. m. However, as a good inductivist, it did not hasten to conclude anything from this. It waited until it had observed many times that it was fed at 9 a.m., and collected these observations under very different circumstances, on Wednesdays and Thursdays, on hot and cold days, on rainy days and on days without rain. Each day, it added another observation statement to its list. Its inductivist consciousness was finally satisfied and it resorted to an inductive inference to conclude: "I am still fed at 9am." Unfortunately, this conclusion proved to be unquestionably false when, on Thanksgiving, instead of feeding it, its head was cut off."

Unfortunately, even if politicians are not or not always stupid (contrary to popular opinion), they still fall a little too often into the trap of the inductivist turkey mindset. And this, despite History which teaches us that the love of the status quo systematically loses the battle against societal "black swans", those unpredictable changes that shake everything up. From Mesopotamia to

---
[2] Alan Chalmers, *What is science?* The paperback book, 1990, page 40

the Roman Empire, from the very holy city of Constantinople to the Indian states of pre-Columbian America, not to mention the French or Bolshevik Revolution in 1917, we see that it is precisely when everything seems under control that the situation degenerates. Very recently we had a clear reminder of this, when in 2011 Mohamed Bouazizi, a local vegetable retailer, no longer able to cope with the grotesque corruption that was suffocating him, killed himself in the village of Ben Arous in Tunisia. This unpredictable act with incalculable consequences, illustrating so well the Lorenz's concept of the "butterfly effect", dear to the followers of the mathematical theory of chaos, provoked what is known as the Arab spring. I myself witnessed it: on a visit to Cairo in January 2010 - a year before Egypt was set ablaze by the fire of regional revolutions - the impression that President Mubarak was there forever was absolute. Of the newspapers singing his glory, the military academies proudly bearing his name, and the population generating tons of praise at him, there is not much left today.

Mubarak, had he become a political inductivist turkey? With all its *mukhabarat* apparatus, omnipresent security services, and the most effective propaganda, did he just shut himself off in the status quo, without paying attention to the signals that society was sending to him? Or, as some analysts claim, were there perhaps no such signals? And was the Tunisian fire of the newly awakened citizen consciousness so rapid, so violent, that the timeframe between the first indicator of future change and the uncontrollable crowd on Tahrir Square frame was much too short to react effectively? It's hard to say. To claim to hold the truth on this subject would be a speculative statement. One thing is certain, however: far from Fukuyama's hallucinations, history is very far from its end. Today, with the more compact world, where the most distant cities are accessible in less than a day, where communication between people is instantaneous and access to knowledge (whatever its quality) is just as instantaneous, it is not just politicians who are challenged, but the very philosophy of governance. All the great challenges facing humanity today are linked to the questions raised by Aristotle and Plato, but for the first time since the emergence of the first societies, these questions are no longer local but global.

Let us take the extremely telling example of Brexit, not unrelated to the demands of the "yellow vests" in France calling for a citizens' initiative referendum, or to the election of Donald Trump with fewer votes than his Democratic rival. The referendum that triggered the United Kingdom's departure from the European Union revealed the incredible crisis of legitimacy that, as we see today throughout the Western world, in a certain way unites all our societies. When on 15 January 2019 the House of Commons voted against the draft agreement between the United Kingdom and the EU presented by Prime Minister Theresa May, the political crisis in the country took the form of a crisis of legitimacy. The multitude of options available for the rest of the affair - between the new referendum, the exit without agreement, or even the cancellation of the pure and simple Brexit - demonstrated to all attentive spectators that, once "business as usual" had become impossible to maintain, the whole political class suddenly realized that it was no longer able to locate the source of its own legitimacy. In 2016, the people voted for Brexit in a referendum that was supposed to be a political maneuver. But in early 2019, following the rejection of the government's proposal on the terms of this unprecedented divorce, who then held the source of all power? The people who voted in 2016 in the "original" referendum? People who would vote in a potential second referendum? Parliament, which votes (de facto) against the clearly expressed will of the people? The government?

This complicated situation, likely to feed the most dangerous populisms ("the elites are still stealing victory from the people" - with a significant reference to the 2005 French referendum on the European constitution) as well as the most beautiful dreams ("true democracy will finally triumph"), would make Karl Hess grin his teeth. For him, it is precisely this type of situation that means the "death" of politics. The presence in the system of governance of intermediary bodies between the will of the people and the implementation of their decisions, these famous "ghosts of the superstitious past", and especially personalities who use questions of capital importance as levers of their own ambitions, was unbearable to him. For the Anglo-Saxon world, used to the very liberal vision of society, this is hardly new. But that the demand for direct popular management now coincides with that of the Nordics or the French visions of the welfare state is, if not unprecedented, at least unexpected for many observers. The democratic "I'm fed up" caused by so many injustices and inequalities, of which Thomas Piketty speaks in his books, returns from time to time to the international spotlight - even to the point of giving birth, in the early 20th century, to the Soviet Union, whose promise of a fairer society had enchanted so many people. How can we forget that the very word "soviet" means nothing other than "council", and that in the governance imagined by Lenin it was precisely these workers' councils that led the communist social structure?

And now the question is back on the table again. And this time, it seems that neither Nozick nor Marx have an answer at the beginning. There are many reasons for this, but probably the first is the incredibly paradoxical nature of the modern world. It is the world of "buts" as never before has humanity known it.

Here is what the American National Intelligence Council said in its report entitled *Paradox of Progress*[3]:

> *"Our ability to cross borders, both physically or digitally, is growing, but we are pushing each other away. Technology has improved our quality of life but has reduced the number of jobs*

---

[3] This report can be downloaded from the NIC website and I can only recommend that you read it: https://www.dni.gov/files/documents/nic/GT-Full-Report.pdf

available in some areas. Governments are still spending more money, but individuals are exercising more power than ever..."

And these are just a few examples.

The changes that affect the way we produce, consume and exchange information inevitably change our relationship to the very concept of power, the future and the meaning. We interact differently at all possible levels; with our friends, co-workers, with the administration; and at all echelons - local, regional, national and international. We have access to so much information - and so many lies! We have so many opportunities to travel and so many reasons not to! *Netflix* becomes, in a way, a competitor of *Air France-KLM*. A minister competes for influence and audience on Facebook with a famous "youtuber". Lobbying today takes place both on Twitter and in the corridors of national parliaments.

Politics is not dead, but it is wounded. The wound is deep, and the French example of the Great National Debate launched by President Macron in January 2019 is very telling: government structures are obliged to invent formats that go beyond constitutional practices, because society, whatever it may be, demands new things. It is organized on social networks that become modern *agoras*, it bypasses representatives because it no longer has confidence, or patience, or both. Private actors, who accumulate wealth beyond all comprehension (the NGO Oxfam reported at the end of January 2019 that the 26 richest individuals now have more money than the poorest half of humanity, or 3.8 billion people), are simply abandoning the legal framework of States, through the solutions that the globalization offers.

This injured politics will recover, but it will no longer be the same. Once healed, it will have to adapt to the new reality that is being built, or that we are building, at this very moment. We have seen, particularly with Brexit and Donald Trump, that despite the (often very sincere) belief in the democratic nature of institutions, these same institutions have been designed to operate within a more or less predictable, or even controllable, framework. When events deviate from the trajectory predicted by the elites - the case of Brexit is very eloquent here - systems derail. One only has to look at the number of times the American specialists have quarreled to decide whether the president could do this or that. Our political systems have shortcomings that become perfectly visible when we take citizen action out of the classic path. This is what hurts politics, makes it vulnerable to populist attacks, and forces it to change.

In the meantime, it is necessary to reset the watches, so they show the correct time. Political science, which has also supposingly "died" in the 1960s, is studying new challenges, but political practice is largely based on tools created for the commercial world, and *success stories* that are not necessarily applicable everywhere. We look for the truth in interviews with Jacques Séguéla, in the work of Jennifer Lees-Marshment, or - for connoisseurs - in the experience of Duda Mendonça, the Brazilian political marketing prodigy who had Lula elected. Experts in "political technologies" are raving about Barack Obama's campaign, and the new European left swears by Bernie Sanders and his Internet successes. The phenomenon, which encompasses all theories and practices that are only aimed at the electoral result, does not belong to the political world itself, but rather to electoral marketing and the management of the image and voters' decision-making. And yet, it is through this same electoral process that "ordinary" people can see the new dynamics that govern 21st century societies. Yet, more and more, the permanent, non-specific nature of this dynamic is becoming apparent. And it is also in this that the wound of politics manifests itself.

In concrete terms, these systemic changes can be attributed to one of the following categories, each with a particular phenomenon in its heart that is unique to our time:

1. **Permanent competition:** life is much less compartmentalized than in the past. As a result, competition between the various elements that compose it transgresses the boundaries between the "domains of life" that were hermetically separated only a few decades ago. Everyone and everything struggle to get our *time* and *attention*, even more than our money, since as consumers we are a valuable resource that others sell and resell. By using

neopolitics

- free of charge at first sight - social networks, for example, it is precisely our time and attention that we offer to the market. And so, a brand-new business was born, a kind of "war of all against all" (hello Hobbes!), or rather, the competition of all against all. It is therefore normal that, in this context, politics itself should become a competitor seeking to capture our attention and that its protagonists should fight against commercial brands. We had already heard the differents Jacques Séguéla explain to us, decades ago, that politicians are brands like any other. At the time, they were only during the elections. Today, they are available 24 hours a day, seven days a week.

2. The **continuous flow of information:** despite their efforts to build a strong and controllable information agenda, politicians no longer have, or have only few "meeting points" with information. The era of the "masters of clocks" is coming to an end. For those who are able, which is quite rare, to control their own message and choose the place and time of its distribution, this message itself is under constant pressure from events, comments and opinions that are, in turn, uncontrollable. Social networks that broadcast around the clock, media scoop hunting, comments and provocations continually influence political communication and blur its signals. It is a form of "forced dialogue" between power and society, a dialogue that never ends, and which, in the end, always escapes from everyone's grasp.

3. **The crisis of personal brands**: it is another paradox. It has never been so easy to push someone to the forefront, thanks to all these means of communication. We went much further than the 15 minutes of glory promised by Andy Warhol: the machine to produce the stars, the Internet also allows us to *remain* a star, if a certain know-how is correctly applied. In politics, this is as true as in show business. A correct proposal, a viral video, a well-found formula can propel anyone to a level of notoriety enough to compete, in the media space, with "established" figures who, in turn, will produce additional credibility for this newcomer. But how not to lose your personality in this so technical space? And how can we really *convince* (I'm not talking about argumentation here, but about the general capacity, all means combined, to find new supporters) in the long term? The "fake news" and the resulting culture of fact checking, the weariness of people in the face of official speeches and at the same time their difficulty in believing honest speech (with rare exceptions like Bernie Sanders), all this creates a dichotomy that makes "ethical positioning" and "respectful technology" gain new importance, never seen before.

And that is where the instruments of neopolitics come into play.

neopolitics

Politics is dead, long live neopolitics

If there is one word that has occupied everyone's mind since the beginning of the century, it is change. Barack Obama embodied it, François Hollande made it his campaign slogan, it is expected in Iran, Russia and Turkey, it comes surprisingly to Brazil, and breaks the codes in Great Britain. The alteration of our lifestyle, which occurred in a decade following the introduction of the iPhone, has almost automatically created an impression of permanent and elusive societal transformation.

Especially since in the modern world, change, the signs of change, are not a political slogan. It does not take a great geopolitical expert to see the rise of tensions in all directions. At first, these tensions may seem cyclical, like the reminiscences of problems known for centuries: immigration, poverty, inequalities... Yet, with the new architecture of information exchange, the new way of communicating, these old problems create new tensions, or reformulate the architecture of old tensions.

Thus, at the national level, citizens return to a basic questioning of what they can expect from their governments. We see it with the "yellow vests", but also in Venezuela or Russia. In the Western world, people are pushing governments to better protect them from crises, and to better ensure their prosperity in the face of an increasingly threatening world.

In turn, these dynamics increase tensions between countries. Europe still handicapped by its divisions, uncertainty about the role of the United States in the world and the weakening of standards of conflict prevention and respect for human rights... All this creates opportunities for China and Russia, but also for sulphurous personalities like Jair Bolsonaro in Brazil. This negative alchemy can also encourage regional and non-state aggressors, fueling regional rivalries, such as the one between Riyadh and Tehran, or between Islamabad and New Delhi, not to mention the Koreas. The possible implosion of Venezuela is creating immense pressure on the countries of the region. Poor governance will also lead to a new perception of threat and insecurity in countries such as Pakistan and North Korea.

For the time being, economic interdependence between the different countries serves as a barrier to interstate conflicts. But, given the increasingly clear trend towards nationalist withdrawal, which is in vogue in Trump's America, but also increasingly openly advocated in European countries such as Italy and Poland, it is easy to imagine a world where this interdependence will no longer be enough. It is not surprising then to see companies making increasingly direct and even violent demands for more stability. Governments must respond in innovative ways, as Emmanuel Macron in France is attempting to do with his Great National Debate, because the rhetoric or violence that might have been sufficient a few decades

neopolitics

ago is no longer able to counter the powerful multipliers of social power that are social networks.

In this context, the terrorist threat - once again, unprecedented in human history because it creates an immediate distortion in the media space - has never been so high. The technical and logistical capacity of terrorist groups to project damage is unprecedented. In addition to the old patterns of convergence with organized crime, the Internet has the potential to recruit, influence and indoctrinate people at a distance, all with very high-quality audiovisual products.

This suggests that, even if states and organizations continue to shape citizens' expectations of future order, their concerns and those of so-called sub-national communities will put increasing pressure on states, so that international and domestic politics will no longer be separable.

So, should we stop talking about politics? Because at least as far as the practice of governance is concerned, whether at the level of a very local community or at the international level, I prefer to speak of *neopolitics* - a new stage in the exercise of power, which is being built every day on an unprecedented and constantly changing basis.

Neopolitics. It was Barbara Cruikshank who introduced this term in her article *Neopolitics: Voluntary Action in the New Regime*[4]. It defines it as "politics in a state

---

[4] in Maasen S., Sutter B., *On Willing Selves*. Palgrave Macmillan, 2007

of adaptation and change". As I find this definition a little too generic, I will go further, even if the concept of change also seems to me - as you have understood - essential. For me, neopolitics means, above all, *the ever-changing architecture of all processes related to political power*, which can be divided into three main parts:

1. What defines political power (*what is the difference between those who have political power and those who do not? In the days of overpowered multinationals and billionaires richer than most states, the question is not so trivial*),
2. How it is accessed (*what are the processes of status changes and obtaining attributes mentioned in question 1, and through which instruments is this change carried out?*), and
3. How to exercise it once you have accessed it (*what are the mechanisms of political decision-making?*)

In view of what has been said above, it would be appropriate to complete these points with the following comments:

1. The current political power ("neopolitical power") is characterized by a mandate given by society, therefore recognized by all social

actors, giving the right to exercise the management of society within the framework defined by the social contract and by using legitimate violence to force the execution of this same mandate. The characteristic of political power is the ability to establish the framework for the exercise of all other types of power (economic, cultural, social...), while no other power can define the framework of political power by order of any kind, although economic power tends to influence political power indirectly;
2. Access to power is achieved by obtaining the above-mentioned mandate, through conviction campaigns targeting those actors in society who can give this mandate in a legitimate and indisputable way. Depending on the society, these actors can vary greatly, but in general and in the Western world we are talking about the population that expresses itself through a vote;
3. Power is exercised within a defined legal framework, and in the context of permanent conviction, through a system of orders and executors. However, the architecture of the framework for the exercise of power also includes limitations that are not established by legislation or tradition.

With this idea of change in mind, politics remains a science, and neopolitics - a set of techniques and knowledge related to political phenomena unique to our time. This means, above all, that by adopting the neopolitical approach, we become aware of the danger of becoming the inductivist turkey. Understanding change means expecting everything every morning at 9 a.m. In addition, I want to emphasize the importance of the word *architecture* that I used earlier: as everything about power changes, from its attributes (the @POTUS Twitter account is the royal scepter of the new age) to its methods, the concept of the new policy must cover *both* the structure of decision-making *and the* ascent to decision-making positions. Thus, politics remains and will always remain, the science of governance, which seeks to understand the nature of power and, as James Holton rightly pointed out earlier, to find ways to improve it for the benefit of humanity. And neopolitics is a body of knowledge on how this governance and its practices are changing in the context of the modern world. And on how to tame them.

This knowledge must have direct applications, that are able respond to concrete situations. It is precisely this toolbox that I mentioned in the introduction to this book. To be effective, they must respond to the three challenges identified in the previous chapter in an efficient manner:

neopolitics

1. Competing effectively with other politicians and other communication actors for attention, support and trust **in order to respond to global and ongoing competition**
2. Build strategies based on continuity, which pursue both strategic and tactical programs, and do not easily allow themselves to be disrupted by "black swan" (i.e. extreme and unpredictable) events, **to survive in the continuity of information flows**
3. Effectively create and manage the personal image (in addition to that of the party, if any), both true to one's personality and easily readable by the public, to extricate oneself from **the crisis of personal brands**

All this, bearing in mind the new elements on which these solutions will be based. Elements that have no real precedent in human history, and thus give the "neo" to neopolitics. Let us mention three of them which are, in my opinion, the most important:

1. The big data,

2. The very rapid change in the role and mode of operation of intermediate bodies of all types (media, society, company, etc.),

3. The new relationship with facts, built on the new applied information philosophy, which I call "neotruth".

In the following chapters, I will first discuss these three changes, these three fundamental facts that form the basis of any neopolitical action. After analyzing them, it will be easy for you to see how the understanding - or misunderstanding - of this new situation has led to the winning or losing of elections, the success or failure of major reforms. Then, armed with this knowledge, we move on to the three categories of tools I have just mentioned. With the increasing use of data, and not only for better target political advertising - we will come back to this in the next chapter - with the ever more direct involvement of people and organizations in processes, and the new paradigm of truth unfolding before our eyes, better instruments are needed to win.

Think of neopolitics as a kind of extra layer in the intellectual scheme of power. As in war, there are bases that do not change, from Lao Tzu to Von Clausewitz, and there are variables that bring new tactical needs, such as gunpowder, aviation, or nuclear weapons. Neopolitics is precisely a word that refers to this new situation, this new "something" that we see happening, whose effects we see, but that we do not fully control. Because the very nature of this "something" is so changing, so volatile, that before we grasp it we must already grasp what chaos theory calls the "strange attractor[5]", this general form that makes it

---

[5] Beautiful definition by Faber Sperber and Robert Paris: the shape of a strange attractor "is not a curve or a surface and is not even continuous but is reconstructed step by step discontinuously by the dynamics which, although apparently disordered, reconstructs this special type of order".

neopolitics

possible to "predict nothing precise", but that draws the framework for the evolution of a system. This little book is only a micro attempt to define this attractor, and I hope that soon, when specialists and political enthusiasts really get down to it, we will really be able to define it.

Data in politics

Data brings changes that affect much more than just the business side of our lives. The amount of information available to companies about *who* we are and *what* we are as social units is so enormous that this data is changing the very fabric of our societies. And, of course, politics, as the basic structure of societal governance, is strongly impacted. But is political data simply a better way to target political announcements? Not really.

In Western democracies, we tend to associate politics with the process of empowerment and the exercise of power. As Chuck Todd and Carrie Dann of *NBC News*[6]

---

[6] The article is entitled *How Big Data Broke American Politics*, from March 14, 2017. Published on NBCNews.com

neopolitics

speculate, big data has "broken" politics, because knowing a lot about those whose votes offer you the desired position - roughly, the customers to whom you sell your services - allows you, just like companies, to target your political campaign so well, that you don't even need to speak to a wider audience. They believe that it is enough to motivate those who are already ready to vote in your favor and to give a little help to those who are hesitant.

Todd and Dann may be wrong, and big data in politics is probably more than just a good way to buy ads on Facebook. Nevertheless, knowing where we spend our time, which series we watch, which books we read, which foods we prefer and which words we are more likely to use in our tweets makes a difference. But what makes politicians "addicted to big data, like if it were campaign money", as *Slate* has titled one their articles? What exactly is the purpose of the data in the policy? Let's try to understand it.

Sherlock Holmes once said (in *A Scandal in Bohemia*): "It is a major mistake to theorize before you have the data. Insensitively, we start twisting facts to adapt them to theories, instead of creating theories and adapting them to facts". This quote dates back to 1891 and yet this "major mistake" is exactly the approach to data, big or small, that people tend to apply today - plus the madness of grandeur.

However, the public authorities have always known its value. As Emily Kumler[7] reminds us, any citizen of ancient Rome who did not show up for the census risked losing his citizenship. After all, the census was a legitimate mean of determining taxes and establishing the social hierarchy of the population. This information was therefore used to ensure better decision-making.

Unfortunately, this "data dependency" has led political actors and their campaign managers to the same illusion that haunts companies: big data, they believe, allows reliable forecasts. Unfortunately, for many of us, the teaching of the mathematical theory of chaos states, among other things, that there are elements of the world so sensitive to the initial conditions that we are technologically incapable of integrating them all into our calculations. This teaching applies very well to the political use of data. The election of Donald Trump was a surprise for data analysts, but not for ordinary people expressing their frustration through the votes and having this "feeling of the field". Similar processes, a kind of return to basics, can be observed in the world of intelligence services, which have invested heavily for years in Echelon-type data analysis systems to discover that what they call HUMINT (for *HUMan INTelligence*), is sometimes much more reliable, and often more important.

---

[7] *The fight for your data is on*, in *Boston Globe* of 9th of July 2017

neopolitics

But this does not mean that collecting and processing metadata in politics is useless. Of course not, of course not. But despite widespread ideas, the most intelligent people do not use them as many journalists and social activists think.

Most people believe - because of the resonance of public scandals such as *Cambridge Analytica* - that big data in politics serves the objectives of better manipulation. That perverse agencies, allied with cynical campaign leaders and why not the Russian government, analyze your behavior in order to better manipulate you in the love of the good candidate and hatred of the bad. This is partly true: indeed, the phenomenon of the "opinion bubble" where people can be placed by better targeting political advertising and thus motivating them to vote and become (without their knowledge) an ambassador of power that has them in its sights, exists. My experience of working with politicians in several countries shows that their actual use of mass data collection and analysis is less about predicting and manipulating future outcomes than about the best analysis of existing ones.

When it comes to public debate, the collection and processing of data on political and social phenomena is almost exclusively associated in the general discourse with the manipulation of votes and Russia's interference in every election there is. Even if it may seem, and rightly so, exaggerated and simplistic, these doubts have triggered the very important questioning by administrations and civil societies.

This questioning is also now in the media. The very famous scenes of Mark Zuckerberg's interrogation in the US Senate have travelled the world's screens. The fact that Facebook and other social networks collect data about us is presented as something outrageous - for example, here is how the report of the UK Information Commissioner's Office's investigation into the use of analytical data in political campaigns, published in November 2018, states the following:

> *"We have concluded that there are risks associated with the processing of personal data by many political parties. Particular concerns include the purchase of marketing lists and lifestyle information from data brokers without due diligence, unfair treatment and the use of third-party data analysis companies, with insufficient controls over consent".*[8]

While in reality, the same problems have existed for years: huge quantities of personal data are sold to companies or collected by the specialized services of the States as part of what they call SIGINT (*Signal Intelligence*). And yet, we only start to panic when we see that the illegal (or barely legal) trade of our life patterns, collected by social networks, has an impact on our political choices.

---

[8] *Investigation Into the Use of Data Analytics in Political Campaigns*, by The British Information Commissioner's Office, page 8

That is indeed a problem. But I think it would be irresponsible to limit our understanding of the influence of data on our socio-political behavior to mere privacy issues. In any case, in the real world, private life is never truly private anymore. The issue of collecting data for the benefit of political actors must not be reduced to mere cynical Frank Underwood-style power brokers, who buy data on what we eat, what we watch on Netflix and who are our friends, to better sell us their promises on how they will improve our lives.

Data in politics is not just a way to target ads. Because we are talking about transactions that are much more complex than simply selling a product with a single value proposition, we must recognize that our data has, in this context, much more than a "one-time" value.

The Berlin-based organization Tactical Tech defines three types of data use in politics, which we will develop further on:

- **Data as political capital**. Valuable reserves of existing data on potential voters exchanged between political candidates, acquired from national repositories or sold or leaked to those who want to exploit them;
- **Data as political intelligence**. Data accumulated and interpreted by political campaigns to identify voters' political preferences and improve campaign strategies and priorities, including the

creation of voter profiles and the testing of campaign messages;
- **Data as political influence**. Data collected, analyzed and used to target and reach potential voters in order to influence or manipulate their views or votes.

Data as political capital

In early June 2017, Hillary Clinton, a former U.S. presidential candidate, delivered a speech at the CODECON conference. She criticized the Democratic Party for its poor data collection skills. "I don't inherit anything from the Democratic Party. I mean, it was a bankruptcy. It was on the verge of insolvency. Its data ranged from poor to non-existent. I had to inject money into it," Clinton said.

For many people, this comment was a revelation: *political parties have data pools!* While in reality, as Emily Kumler, an American entrepreneur mentioned above, puts it, there is a "hypothesis that we have accepted the use of scientific methods specifically designed to mislead us, to reinforce the fears and alliances that we already have, without any responsibility, as a condition of our current political process". Because, yes, data pools exist and are used as an asset in political transactions - and yes, we expressly consent to them every day, using our favorite services. They are collected by third parties and sold to entities participating in the elections. In Europe, where the political systems of most countries allow a more diversified offer than the American bipartisan convention, new parties and movements are sometimes created for the sole reason of collecting data from a certain type of voters, and sellim them later to larger actors.

Data of the "political capital" type are not used directly. They are exchanged between candidates, sold and bought in transactions between different players in the political sector. They can also serve as leverage during negotiations, for example by exposing different quantified scenarios to competitors.

This type of data may include, but is not limited to:

- **Political data strictly speaking** (database of voters in the United States, for example, but also party membership info, data collected during intra-party surveys, as well as data from so-called canvassing software that groups people into political strata for campaign purposes). This data is collected directly by the parties and/or their suppliers;
- **Consumer data** (lifestyle and consumption habits, up to geolocation and travel). They come from commercial sources, who sell them;
- **Public registry data**. Collected on the Internet via open sources, they are then collected and sold to political actors;

- **The leaks**. Databases concerning the target electorate that are leaked. Unfortunately, examples exist everywhere, from Africa to Canada.

Data as political intelligence

Some types of data, such as your psychological profile, are almost not used to target ads. Rather, they help decision-makers in their daily work of adjusting ongoing - or planned - activities. In an election campaign, this "intelligence" type of data allows an effective grouping of target audiences.

For an incumbent politician, having up-to-date information on different segments of the population makes it easier to consider the possible response to a public decision. No need to go far to find a good example: the turmoil of early 2019 with Donald Trump in a deadlock with Congress on his wall on the southern border of his country is an excellent case study showing how data strengthen decision-making. The White House team, which, as the *Cambridge Analytica* episode proves, is in love with big data, would never decide on a public message from the Oval Office without having a very deep insight into the many cohorts of the American population. The message to this population was designed to strengthen Trump's central electorate, to sow the seeds of doubt in the minds of those who have no strong position and to exalt democrats to do or say something stupid. That being said, it did not work.

It is impossible to even start trying to build this type of political action today without information about the audience receiving the message.

But this type of data is also used in internal power sets. When you make, for example, staff-related decisions, you may tend to use data to justify the dismissal or hiring of a certain person. In difficult negotiations with political opponents, having data on your voters can be a crucial argument. This also works at the international level. President Trump is remembered for mentioning, in one of his tweets, the weak support given to Emmanuel Macron by the French population as a geopolitical argument.

Thus, intelligence-type data are those collected and used for "digital listening" to improve political or campaign decision-making. If we imagine that you are the target of this type of collection, here are the different types of information that can constitute political intelligence:

- **What kind of person you are**. This data is collected and analyzed in order to define your values, your motivations - and which may provoke the expected response from you. These include the results of various psychometric tests, such as OCEAN (which define your personality type sometimes without you knowing it, following your use

of Facebook for example - IBM Watson artificial intelligence already allows it for example), and all the other behavioral data that is available about you;
- **Your interests**. This is the data collected when you surf the web and use applications on your smartphones and computers, with the aim of better understanding your habits, behavior, hobbies etc. You generate this data using *cookies*, files that analyze your behavior on the sites, and the various analysis mechanisms that are part of the architecture of the applications used;
- **What you are talking about online**. This is what we mean when we use the term "digital listening". It is well known that Facebook, for example, analyzes not only the messages sent and posted, but also those that you started writing but then deleted. Semantic analysis of your posts, tweets, messages on social networks and forums provides this type of data;
- **What you respond to**. Mass checks of different types of narration, different messages, visuals etc.: these are the data generated largely by your interactions with advertisements (which one did you click on? which one did you ignore? which one did you hesitate to click on, and for how long did you have your mouse pointer on it?). Today, there are even ads generated by algorithms, to better

respond to the way you become interested in something.

Data as political influence

That's the part everyone's talking about. The data used to directly influence our decision. And we're not just talking about "Vote for me" banners appearing in the middle of your Instagram feed. Depending on your profile and the goals set by the campaign team, you may, for example, see a message on the horrible long lines at the polling station in your district that will discourage you from actually going there and casting your vote. And these messages will appear to come from a legitimate news outlet, unrelated to any candidate: unlike the legal directives on television, online advertising basically has no obligation to disclose the paying entity.

And while in the EU the momentum is shifting towards stronger and more restrictive regulation of this type of practice, the United States' and, for example, the African online advertising markets remain extremely liberal.

Once again, let us imagine that you are the voter so sought after by political actors. What kind of information can help them influence you, and with what instruments?

- Knowing **who you are** can help to better target ads and so-called *dark posts* (advertising publications made in the form of sponsored post that are made by specifying that the publication should not be displayed on the brand page - of the party, the politician... - and among its subscribers). It also allows you to send you personalized emails, and place ads up to in the games you play on your smartphone;
- Knowing **where you are** allows you to set up what is called geofencing or georeferencing: creating virtual barriers for your gadgets. This allows to show you ads based on your location and improve online political prospecting and canvassing;
- Being aware of what **you are looking for** can logically optimize the content of political websites, with what is called SEO (*search engine optimization*) and sometimes *black hat SEO*, i.e. SEO techniques that violate certain rules of search engines;
- **What you read and watch online** opens the door, without any surprises, to the micro-targeting of political advertising that will get into your playlists on YouTube, for example;
- Having access to **your contact lists, i.e.** knowing who you know, allows canvassing software to access your networks, influence you through the people you follow on these social networks, and - as we have seen in the United States - create message strategies based on community criteria and

statistics generated by applications like Messenger or even Tinder;

And it should not be forgotten that new technologies are constantly being tested in order to improve this power of influence. Largely based on artificial intelligence, they are used in most cases to meet two main needs: automate political marketing and improve communication through solutions such as chatbots. In the neopolitical world where, as I mentioned earlier, competition is permanent, never ceases and becomes every day more and more global, the need to be present and competitive well beyond the occasional electoral deadlines explains these needs.

And it works?

It is possible to have a somewhat paranoid reaction to this list of the different scrutinies we are all under while we are using our dear online services. However, these methods, tools and approaches are only the translation into modern means of the wills of control and analysis that have existed since the birth of human society. It is a societal and technological reality that can be denied as much as you like, but that remains real, and that nothing seems to be able to disturb. Whether it is a democratic disaster or, on the contrary, a springboard for a new development of our societies, depends on how we use these technologies. As Kate Dommett, Director of the Crick Center at the University of Sheffield, states, "Digital campaign tools can help parties win elections, but they also have important side effects on the way democracy works. If societies value equality of information, open debate and transparency, these trends should be of concern. But if the focus is rather on engaging voters on the issues and ideas that interest them (campaigns targeting at the most basic level), new practices may be less worrying."

As I mentioned earlier, in Europe the limits imposed on data collection and processing companies are generally stricter than elsewhere, in particular through the GDPR (General Data Protection Regulation) mechanism, active since 2018 in the Union. However, this does not mean that the substance of political activities in the EU is different from what we have mentioned above – it is just somewhat adapted to the local legal limits. For example, in France, the American political campaign software company *NationBuilder*, used by three presidential candidates in 2017, had to disable a data collection feature that did not comply with the directives of the CNIL (*Commission nationale de l'informatique et des libertés*, which ensures that privacy rules are respected). But this action took place only seven weeks before the elections. We are talking about the "Correspondence" feature, which is normally enabled by default, and allows campaigns to cross-reference voters' public account

neopolitics

information from Facebook, LinkedIn, Twitter and Meetup.com related to email addresses provided on the campaign website (for example, following subscriptions to a candidate's newsletter). The company could then integrate the data of any Internet user who liked one of the campaign-related Facebook or Twitter posts. In some cases, the location and biography of users, as provided in the accounts, were also stored. *NationBuilder* pretends having helped its customers to eliminate incorrectly collected data, the volume of which remains unknown.

In November 2016, the CNIL investigated Knockin[9], an application developed and used by the right-wing party *Les Républicains* primary campaign of presidential candidate Nicolas Sarkozy. The application identified and geolocated Sarkozy supporters for a door-to-door campaign. The solicitors then visited the electors' homes according to the map created by the application, and addressed these people by name. Something a part of the voters found, not surprisingly, invasive. An investigation revealed that, without the voters' knowledge, simply liking Sarkozy's Facebook page or one of his Twitter messages described the voter as "regular contact", thus allowing the campaign to collect the voter's public data (voter registration, Facebook, Twitter, LinkedIn, etc.). Despite this, however, the CNIL declared the application perfectly legal, with a subsequent declaration stating that

---

[9] As reported, for example, by the *Nouvel Obs* of 17 November 2016

combining date relating to voters from different sources could not be done without consent.

In countries where data protection rules are, let us say, more flexible, the use of information from all types of voters is now almost limitless. For example, in Kenya, the August 2017 elections were[10] in some ways a test field for the abovementioned techniques. In these elections all parties used professional campaign consultants specialized in data tech. And we are not only talking about local consultants and influencers, but also about international companies such as *Cambridge Analytica* (United Kingdom), *Aristotle, Inc.* or *Harris Media* (United States). They provided services ranging from "negative campaigning" (or as it is sometimes called, "black PR") to the creation and dissemination of viral content, hashtags and "likes" for selected groups of supporters and voters - targeting made possible by a variety of stratification measures.

However, although impressive, the results show that purely digital campaigns are not enough to win an election. A huge number of serious researches were conducted in the United States following the 2016 elections to understand the role played by social networks (and, by extension, the influence campaigns launched from

---

[10] See the very complete report by Grace Mutung'u for Tactical-Tech, which can be downloaded for free at https://ourdataourselves.tacticaltech.org/media/ttc-influence-industry-kenya.pdf

neopolitics

Russia). And basically all of these researches, like those conducted by the Columbia School of Journalism or Harvard, are, in the words of Nick Clegg[11], former British Deputy Prime Minister and now responsible for Facebook's public affairs, "very clear on one point": they say that the traditional media have played the most important role. The importance of television remains enormous, even in societies where the screen of the smartphone is infinitely more important than that of the TV set in the living room. But the trend is clear: the weight of data in politics will become increasingly important, and platforms such as Civis (which brings together the data of more than 200 million Americans used for political purposes) will flourish. And we all, actors or spectators of political life, must find our place in this new neopolitical world.

---

[11] In *Le Monde*, January 28, 2019. It should be noted that even if the researches do confirm this point of view, Mr Clegg is, by virtue of his new position, somewhat biased

igor lys

Intermediate Bodies and Participative Democracy in Neopolitics

In a book entitled *Myth and Reality of the Legitimacy Crisis: Explaining Trends and Cross-National Differences in Established Democracies*, published by Oxford University, a plethora of brilliant researchers (Carolien van Ham, Jacques Thomassen, Kees Aarts, and Rudy Andeweg) draws our attention to the fact that, at least since the 1960s (discussed at the beginning of the book), the concept of the crisis of representative democracy returns, without really changing anything in the end in our understanding of its role in our societies. This crisis, which is also that of the legitimacy of the representative

neopolitics

bodies in general, be them governmental, economic, trade union or other, seems to be firmly rooted in people's minds. Whether it's the experts at the Saturday night bistro or the big names in science. For example, one of the first to shout it out was Jürgen Habermas[12]. A little earlier, in 1959, Lipset became a kind of precursor of Fukuyama by announcing no less than "the end of ideology" following the possible erasing of the various political divisions linked to the ever-increasing level of education which should produce *disengaged* citizens, and consequently, the disappearance of representative democracy due to a lack of voters.

The reality of today of which van Ham and company speak is therefore not really new, although the technological advancements and changes listed at the beginning of this book add new elements within the framework of the well-known equations. In all societies with a democratic tradition, there is a kind of fundamental question that keeps appearing in response to the gap between announcements and reality: does "*the real-existing democracy*" meet citizens' expectations? Knowing that these expectations are formulated for a perfect democracy that differs from the one we "experience" in the real world, which remains despite all the only one that offers us tangible effects.

The answer would be rather negative. Polls and studies of all kinds go in this direction, and without going

---

[12] His book *Legitimationsprobleme im Spätkapitalismus*, very influential at the time, was published in 1973

that far, we can all see the societal and electoral dynamics pushing anti-system parties and candidates to the top of power. The Trump, Brexit or Bolsonaro phenomena prove that the trend is clearly towards growing mistrust of democratic mechanisms. Yet, barely a century ago, we saw worse! And democracy had returned, despite everything, having, on its way, destroyed the alternative models proposed by Nazi Germany and the USSR. In what way would the current trend be more serious, less cyclical, than previous ones? What is so different in the neopolitical world that the question of the crisis of representativeness, in governance structures and elsewhere, is being raised like never before? I think that one of the great differences lies in the technological revolution which, slowly but surely, removes, piece by piece, the very utility - or, to be more precise, the perception of utility - of intermediate bodies.

Yascha Mounk is a political scientist, Harvard professor and member of the Tony Blair Institute for Global Change. He is also the author of an important book called *The People Against Democracy*[13]. Published one year after van Ham et al.'s book, this work highlights the dangers that weigh on the representative system today, and gives very precise explanations, which are in line with the points mentioned on the previous pages. Apart from the economic question (which, roughly speaking, means that

---

[13] *Le peuple contre la démocratie*, in French. Editions of the Observatory, 2018

neopolitics

for the first time in a very long time the wealth and quality of life in non-democratic countries have caught up with those in Western countries, which in turn can no longer guarantee future generations a standard of living necessarily higher than the one their parents had), another important feature is mentioned by Mounk. The emergence of social networks, these great disrupters in the way, on the one hand, to create the agenda, and on the other hand, to organize social actions. In an interview[14], Mounk explains:

> *"[Social networks] have a double effect. First, to remove the monopoly of opinion from the elites. If you look at the way the major news channels operated fifteen years ago, the editorial offices spotted what was happening in the world, decided which theme should be on the front page and people discussed what they had seen on the news. The roles are now reversed. People keep up with what's happening in the world on Facebook and Twitter, and the topics they talk about the most make a topic on the primetime.*
>
> *The second major change is the organization of the protest. Until recently, it was organized by a political party or trade union which issued a call with a date, a place of protest and prepared buses to bring the demonstrators. Today, you can*

---

[14] In *Le Monde*, the January 30, 2018 edition

see an event set up chaotically and spontaneously on Facebook lead to a viral mobilization. This raises new questions for governments because, if they know how to negotiate with an angry union, they have no idea how to manage a horizontal and leaderless mobilization."

It is easy to see that the two phenomena are not simply linked, but present both sides of the same categorical and unprecedented change: for the first time in human history, a technological solution has replaced human beings as the organizer of their efforts. This brings about a major change: whereas when the organization (whatever its nature) is managed by a person, it is he who, directly or indirectly, oversees its agenda. A digital platform, on the other hand, is completely neutral in the sense that it merely provides the logistics tools accessible to everyone.

Those whom Mounk calls the elites, that social stratum that is responsible for the general direction of the development of society, have always been very vigilant in keeping this control of the agenda. Any attempt to unbalance it in any way, whether it was the Spartacus rebellion or the May 68 uprising, had to be stopped, punished and then analyzed in order to make its repetition impossible. Between the massacre of 11,000 slaves and the division of Parisian universities, this *modus operandi*, this protocol has not changed. Until the emergence of social networks.

neopolitics

It was with the Arab Spring that specialists began to take a serious interest in this new type of dynamic, born not of a structured call but of a series of reactions often without a real plan, difficult to recover and unpredictable in their implementation[15].

Research conducted in the years following the events on the role of social networks and the Internet in general in the success of this popular movement has produced surprising results, important for understanding the multimodal power that networks provide to action groups. At first, a kind of consensus emerged among researchers on the critical importance of online services in generating and managing protest crowds, as well as in synchronizing claims[16]. But then new discoveries were made. In July 2012, the highly respected United States Institute of Peace published a report based on an in-depth analysis of the content of *bit.ly* links resulting from the uprisings in Tunisia, Egypt, Libya and Bahrain. *Bit.ly* links, or shortened URLs, are mainly used in social media such as Twitter. The authors reached conclusions that complemented the initial hypothesis that social media was a "causal" mechanism in uprisings. In particular, the study suggests that the importance of social networks also

---

[15] Some, such as the American Michael Hyatt, trace its origins to the Iranian elections of 2009. But even if, at the time, Twitter had indeed played a key role in information sharing, speaking of the horizontal organization of networked protests would be incorrect regarding this election

[16] Cf. par exemple *The Role of Digital Media*, article par Howard, Philip and Muzammil M. Hussain. in *Journal of Democracy*. Juillet 2011.

lay in communicating to the rest of the world what was happening on the ground during the uprisings. "New media using *bit.ly* links are more likely to disseminate information outside the region than inside, acting more like a megaphone than a rallying cry," the study said[17]. Thus, social networks have become the new media in every sense of the word.

Since then, with the big data mentioned above, the strengthening of algorithms, the ever-increasing penetration of the Internet in the most remote villages, history has given dozens of examples of the increasingly serious use of new technologies to circumvent the millenary rules of social organization. Between the *Occupy* movement, the success of the *Podemos* party in Spain and the success of Bernie Sanders' campaign in the United States, the protests on Bolotnaya Square in Moscow and - the height of this decentralization of protest logistics - the "yellow vests" in France, the emancipation of intermediate bodies offered by technology is increasing day by day.

The same book you are reading is proof of this: accessible through sales platforms without any institutional publisher having a say, it certainly does not benefit from the media clout of publishing houses and literary agents. But he nevertheless finds his reader through an online

---

[17] The study is entitled *Blogs and Bullets II: New Media.* Aday, Sean, Henry Farrell, Marc Lynch, John Sides, and Deen Freelon. It can be downloaded from the USIP website, http://www.usip.org/files/resources/PW80.pdf

communication campaign, mixing genres and perfectly autonomous.

In this perspective, it is interesting to see that in Russia in recent years, personal blogs (including posts on Facebook and Twitter) have been legally considered as media starting from a certain number of subscribers, thus signaling legal equality between a major newspaper and a major youtuber. While bloggers (and it must be said that in Putin's country blogs, especially those hosted on the LiveJournal platform, are very popular since they represent an important opening of freedom of expression) see this as an infringement of their freedom of speech, the traditional media are concerned that their status as a monopoly of information sources is being undermined in terms of legislation. This is exactly what Mounk was talking about: the elites can no longer really control the agenda. We will see later, in the chapter on permanent competition, what implications this has for the acquisition and exercise of political power.

Thus, is the undeniable increase in this protest activity one of the symptoms of the evil that our democracy is experiencing? Van Ham and his colleagues explain in their book that the crisis as such does not really exist, although the perception is very real and, in a way that is difficult for researchers to understand, "resistant to evidence" provided by scientists[18].

---

[18] *Myth and Reality of the Legitimacy Crisis.* Carolien van Ham, Jacques Thomassen, Kees Aarts, Rudy Andeweg, Oxford University Press, 2017. Cf. chapitre 11

But we know that neopolitics, that is, the practice of real governance in a world where the architecture of power is constantly changing, can be, and often is, out of step with politics as a science. Politicians have to deal more with facts, including people's "psychological reality", than with theories. People do not always act rationally, and decision-makers do not have time to be surprised that something did not go as planned. They must act to prevent or manage crises, carry out reforms, prepare for their re-election or undermine the efforts of competitors. All this in a real world where things happen as they happen. And in this world, the democratic crisis is a "psychological reality", or "inner empirical reality", that is, people act as if it were real because it is real in their heads. As a result, supported in their efforts by errors of analysis, media manipulation and ultimately by the phenomenon of self-fulfilling prophecy, citizens are seeking to close the gap in what they consider to be the failure in their governance system, even if the real failure may lie elsewhere. This is symptomatic for almost all democratic or proto-democratic societies, and unlike centuries and centuries of similar crises, it now brings concrete results in almost all countries where elections had taken place in recent years.

Emmanuel Macron who destroys the French political landscape established for decades, Donald Trump

neopolitics

who leaves the most imperturbable commentators in his country stunned, Brexit who brings with it the almost total loss of democratic control on the basis of slogans such as "take back control", Brazil, which puts in the presidential chair a man who swears only by the destruction of the current system... If books much thicker than this one try and will continue to try for a very long time to solve these cases, trying to explain the reasons, the question that interests me in the neopolitical context of these events is: how did all this become possible? Why, in recent years, is such a change no longer really surprising? No matter what the substance of the programs implemented by the new managers is: they are very different and are generated mainly in very different societal settings. It is not their causes or outcomes that unite these changes - but their mechanisms.

And among all, the one that the Arab Spring was the first to reveal in the open: the marginalization of intermediate bodies.

This marginalization is possible thanks, on the one hand, to this feeling of imminent or ongoing crisis - a feeling that, although contradicting political scientists, is perceptible in all opinion surveys on all continents, - and on the other hand, to the horizontality of social communication that social networks and other digital solutions, such as the FireChat application (which makes it possible to create communication networks by Bluetooth and therefore in the absence of a mobile network that can be cut by the authorities).

The crisis agenda is not something specific to our time. But before, it was most often initiated by pressure groups as a means of creating a certain social and political capital, since the theme of decadence (in any form whatsoever: corruption, laxity, etc.) is very promising in this extent. It can almost always be projected on a "small reality" of the daily life of the working and middle classes, whatever the country and whatever the political system. The success of all the crises generated and managed within such a paradigm proves it. Between Ancient Greece and contemporary China, the logic of maintaining this state of alert is perfectly understandable, because it allows the generation of a mobilization that can bring about either political and social change or, conversely, so-called stability, which, if properly managed, can bring (or maintain) the instigators of the crisis to power. The real interest of a crisis thus generated therefore lay in most cases either in weakening an opponent (and then hitting him or offering him support) or in recovering the political capital generated by a mass movement.

However, this mechanism only makes sense if the agenda, the cause that motivates the movement (whether generated by random events or artificially designed), is if not defined, then at least recovered by an intermediate body that carries a message and manages the corresponding social and political capital. To the extent that a movement does not have this external "cause management", it disintegrates while retaining a recognizable and unifying symbolism. The "yellow vest" movement in France is a

neopolitics

very good example of this: born of a project to protest the increase in fuel taxes, it has become a heterogeneous phenomenon that is only united by the very symbol of the famous vest. Without real leadership, a movement like the "yellow vests" or *Occupy* could not persist in the political world as we have imagined it for centuries. But neopolitics makes, begins to make this possible.

Social networks, by replacing people-rules organizations and institutions managed by people, somehow neutralize the verticality of the social thing. By proposing technical solutions that make it possible to have media exposure comparable to that of "real" politicians (i.e. recognized by the "classic" media as the spokespersons for a particular social trend), Facebook, Twitter and YouTube mark the beginning of a media *equivalence* between the world of "opinion leaders" and the "common people" who, using their smartphones, a coherent speech and possibly a little luck become legitimate members of the public mass media space.

In an interview with *Il Manifesto in* September 2018, Professor Noam Chomsky explained his vision of societal dynamics in the United States and Europe, which he said was the result of the appropriation by the "elites" of increasingly important benefits. According to Chomsky, the fact that real wages (especially in the United States) are at their lowest level in decades, as well as the right-hand shift made by leaders, even those claiming to be from the left, push people to seek easy solutions. To this rather unoriginal statement, the famous intellectual adds two important and, let us dare to say, neopolitical things: the first is the refusal to qualify the dynamics mentioned as "populist" (for Chomsky, it is not a populist manipulation but a legitimate desire of the people to revolt against inequalities), and the second is the possible emergence of new candidates driven by new technologies on the one hand, and by the rejection of the current system on the other hand. The example he gives is Bernie Sanders. "The most remarkable feature of the 2016 campaign, says Chomsky, was not the election of a billionaire, who had huge funds, especially in crucial end-of-campaign phases, and enormous media support... The most remarkable element is Sanders' campaign, which breaks with more than a century of American political history in which elections are predictable with remarkable precision, which is also true for Congress... It is enough to compare the campaign spending to understand it." Further on, the "spiritual father of the American left", as some call him, develops his thinking by explaining precisely how this emergence was possible thanks to the direct communication of the candidate with his electorate, and this, with budgets infinitely smaller than those of the "big" candidates. "Sanders was almost unknown, had been dismissed or ridiculed by the media, had no funding from business or private wealth, and even used the word "socialism", a terrifying word in the United States, unlike other companies," says Chomsky. And yet, here he is - at least for the duration of an election - one of the most popular political figures in the country.

Of course, the intermediate bodies do not disappear. But their role is changing, and their weight is decreasing. Interestingly, this desire for horizontal social relations, this tendency to eliminate intermediaries of all kinds, was officially formulated and attempted during the French Revolution. In 1791, Le Chapelier said: "There is no longer a corporation in the State; there is only the particular interest of each individual and the general interest. No one is allowed to inspire citizens with an intermediate interest, to separate them from the public domain by a corporate spirit". You'd think those words came directly from Bolsonaro's mouth. As Professor Pierre Rosanvallon pointed out in his lecture at the Collège de France, at the time, this desire to eliminate all social mediation was above all a way of preventing the polarization of society and thus ensuring the cohesion of the nation. This nation must then be, according to Rosanvallon's formula, "irreducible to any intermediate component whatsoever". In the neopolitical world, on the other hand, it is precisely polarization that is at the root of this new dynamic. Technologies that allow people to gather without providing judgement or direct influence on the agenda, which were absent in the 18th century, open a new avenue to the demands of minorities of active people and therefore capable of projecting actions that shake up the functioning of society at all levels. These actions can take very different forms. In the context of the perceived crisis mentioned above, there is a framework for transforming economic and social frustrations into simplistic solutions, dangerous projections but also the necessary balances, which can be achieved through actions designed and implemented on horizontal platforms.

Defined a long time ago by Montesquieu and recently clarified by political scientist Yves Mény[19], the *raison d'être* of intermediate bodies (in France - but this is also true for the concept *per se*) was to represent groups that have a common interest before decision-makers in the respective field. Not only politically, this phenomenon found very diverse applications, for example the soviets in Bolshevik Russia, or the English principle of *government by committee*. Mény proposes the classification into 3 types: political-social organizations (political parties, trade unions, employers...), sectoral professional organizations (chambers of commerce, chambers of agriculture, bar association) and associations. It is mainly the first two that interest us. In the neopolitical world, with the changes mentioned above, but also with a whole series of almost daily technological changes, these elements of society are losing power[20].

---

[19] See in particular the *Constructive* Review #30, November 2011.
[20] I am embarking here on a difficult exercise of generalizing change without looking at the socio-political context of a particular country or industry. I hope you will therefore forgive me for a certain lack of precision, the objective here being to explain the trends rather than to define the concrete quantifiable changes.

neopolitics

Political and social organizations coexist now with ephemeral groups, existing only for the duration of a Facebook event, while their structural and structured competitors can emerge more easily than ever. However, these organizations are not losing their importance, but they are now evolving in a much more volatile context. On the one hand, the emergence of new actors is facilitated by technology (the current ruling party in France, *La République en marche*, was created *ad hoc* for the 2017 elections, and yet has an absolute majority in the National Assembly), and on the other hand, they compete with proto-organizations such as "yellow jackets", existing only on social networks and on the streets and outside any traditional framework (authorities, legal entities, statutes, local...). It is relatively certain that these new types of horizontal proto-organizations are one of the major drivers of change. Thanks to digital platforms, whether established social networks or communities created for a specific cause (such as the *En Marche!* movement that gave birth to Emmanuel Macron's party we've just mentioned, or Bernie Sanders' website during his campaign), it is possible to compete with established parties because technical solutions replace experience, expertise and logistics previously inaccessible to independents.

Sectoral professional organizations must understand that the relationship between the worker and the organization is forever changed

because of social networks. By giving a voice, and therefore a media existence, to an individual as much as to an organization, they allow anyone to "jump" over classic hierarchies in the classic protocol of protest. Nicolas Stoop, then community manager of Medef (French union of corporate leaders), said in 2011 that "social networks are, basically, only an aggregate of individualisms without logic or collective strategy deliberately thought out and reflected as such, whereas professional unions, if they are based on taking into account the individualities that belong to them, retain a large degree of centralization in determining their most important strategy or actions", and that they cannot therefore "replace, in order to defend the general interest of a category of the population, structured organizations which would nevertheless have an interest in making the best use of them"[21]. We now know how much impact can, for example, a message about a case of harassment posted on Twitter have on a company's stock market value. And we have seen on many occasions how new technologies either upset the trade union landscape where they are present, or give workers opportunities in the contexts where trade unions do not have the same role as we have in France (I am thinking in particular of Russia or China). For example, corporate social networks (also known as private social networks) "flatten" the hierarchy of employees' internal communication, allowing management to bypass union presence and

---

[21] In *Constructive* #30.

neopolitics

communicate directly with all employees. At the same time, employees can communicate directly with management. Of course, in the case of Asian countries, for example, the Internet has not yet been able to influence the condition of the working class, except in China, through the creation of an Orwellian surveillance system. But in the West, networks and the web allow unions and workers to act in new ways.

It would be easy - and tempting! - to say that the Internet and social networks provide solutions above all for the development of intermediate bodies rather than weakening them. Aren't corporate Intranet networks a wonderful tool for unions? Don't targeted advertising campaigns and instant communication on Twitter allow NGOs of all kinds to better explain their work and raise more funds? Yes, of course they are and they do. In the conflict that broke out in 2011 at the British East Lindsey refinery, for example, much of the protest organization was carried out via websites and SMS messaging. This allowed a local conflict to spread overnight to more than 20 other industrial sites across the country. In addition, the websites created by workers have generated much broader support, going beyond that of union members - making the union almost marginal in its own struggle[22]. The conflict itself involved several hundred workers from other European countries who came to work at the

---

[22] Case reported by Stuart Smith, CEO of Wood Holmes

refinery. They were housed on a barge where they were largely confined outside working hours. Normally, the influx of temporary workers on the site would have stimulated the local economy, but as this was not the case, hoteliers, shop owners and caravan park owners added their support to the conflict via the website set up by the union. So new technologies do not automatically mean that the intermediate bodies disappear.

But the speech equivalence provided by Twitter and Facebook makes it very fragile for organizations to dominate people's objectives. Especially in Anglo-Saxon countries. According to many commentators, after the emergence of the political and social rights movement in the same 1960s and 1970s that we mentioned at the very beginning (and whose *modus operandi* was above all collective action through strikes), we are now reaching the priority of the exercise of individual rights. However, will it lead to the new, network-based actions of the existing structures, or do social media usher in a new era in which "individuals" are organized collectively through these tools *without* a corresponding legal body, in order to give leaders a way to hear the voices of the governed? And do the networks offer a new credible mechanism for intermediate bodies to succeed and demonstrate their strength? One thing is certain: if, on the one hand, they effectively allow the different types of institutional intermediaries to better broaden their base and focus their efforts, on the other hand they make it difficult (and often impossible) to identify the decision-makers' interlocutors, create "digital crowds" united by the same brand but which do not necessarily share the same objectives, and above all, give unprecedented power to the voices of individuals without necessarily providing these voices a stable base. People who propel a stranger from yesterday onto the front pages of newspapers with their likes and reposts can be just as effective in forgetting as they are in generating this notoriety 2.0.

It is precisely this unpredictable aspect of the new way of acting as a group, of which only the contours are defined, that gives the "neo" to today's political practice. This was clearly seen in the management by Emmanuel Macron's teams of the beginning of the yellow vest crisis in France. He has been seen in the digital initiatives of Vladimir Putin's chief opponent, Alexei Navalny, which sometimes work (like his calls to demonstrate against corruption in the country), and sometimes don't (like his digital platform which, by analyzing the poll data, proposes to vote - in regional elections - for the anti-party candidate in power who has the best chance of winning).

As is the case with big data, we must not get too excited: big data does not (yet) win elections, just as the drastic change in the relationship with intermediate bodies does not yet shake up all the world's political agendas. But if we begin to analyze trends rather than facts first, we will arrive at a series of important conclusions that, in a neopolitical universe, will influence the way governance is exercised:

1. **Intermediate bodies have lost the monopoly on representing people's interests**. Technological solutions replace organizations, giving, on the one hand, the capacity of horizontal organization, and on the other hand, the unequalled media power;
2. **The temporality of the intermediate bodies has also changed**: in addition to the pursuit of major causes and, occasionally, local causes (protest against a law or a factory closure, support for a victim of police violence, etc.), there are spontaneous events, often on almost random subjects,
3. And finally - and this is probably the most important trend - these changes, which are beginning to be perceived by more and more people, and "tested" by more and more communities, are beginning to change the very lines of **people's perception of the political world**. Seeing the tools of direct management, organization and mediatization in action inspires people to want, according to the unfortunate slogan of the pro-Brexit campaign, to "regain control".

Here the decline, true or imagined, of participatory democracy (especially since participation has been declining steadily for years in many Western countries) coincides with the rise of citizens' initiatives, and the feedback that people give to public authorities only confirms the inevitability of future changes in the Western democratic machinery. In France, the Big Debate - a series of citizen consultations - launched by Emmanuel Macron as one of the responses to the "yellow vest" crisis, is sometimes seen as a clever invention, but in reality, it is only a way of applying what has long been advocated by a whole range of experts who carefully analyze the dynamics of the relationships between people and the bodies that are supposed to represent them. For example, Arne Pautsch, Professor of Local and Governmental Law at Ludwigsburg University in Germany, was writing already in 2017:

"The so-called crisis of representative democracy will become more and more chimerical when the instruments oriented towards dialogue and the procedures of citizen participation, consultation and deliberation are effectively used for consultation and deliberation. In this context, citizen participation - especially if applied at the local level - is a valid way to improve the democratic system, which will thus consist of participatory democracy as its main pillar, direct democracy and - as a new supplement - citizen participation-oriented dialogue as the third pillar, encompassing in a way the others[23]".

---

[23] *The assumed crisis of representative democracy and the role of citizen participation in Germany.* Arne Pautsch. 2017, University of Ludwigsburg (published in English). For German speakers, see also the book published in 2016: *Die Konsultative - Mehr Demokratie durch Bürgerbeteiligung*. Patrizia Nantz, Claus Leggewie. 2016, Nanz & Leggewie.

Thus, what specialists have been talking about for years is being achieved almost despite the will of the leaders, and we are only at the very beginning of this process. Interaction, dialogue and inclusion are today the main opportunities, but also the main challenges, of the "art of the possible". Driven by the perception of the societal crisis that comes to life following this self-fulfilling prophecy, the *passionnarii*, these people with the "long will" as defined by the great Russian ethnographer and historian Lev Goumiliov, obtain a striking power comparable with the largest unions or parties. Integrating this power into the arsenal of existing structures is an important challenge that neopolitical strategists will be able to meet tomorrow - if we start the necessary preparatory work today.

neopolitics

The Neotruth

"You are fake news!". This sentence, initially Donald Trump's personal trademark, has established itself as a kind of banal, yet very fashionable commentary on everything and anything. Only the laziest of political journalists and the laziest of political scientists did not express themselves on this era of "post-truth" in which we would all be enveloped.

But these paradigms that seem new to us, thanks to all these new and so catchy terms, must not become victims of the incessant speculation that they themselves constantly denounce. Thus, in order to be able to speak about neopolitics, it is crucial to put the points on the i's with regard to new relationships to facts, truth and information in general. Indeed, how can we talk about political brands, elections, power and influence, without mentioning the very heart of society: communication between its members?

We have seen that big data serve as leverage and instruments for political actors. We have understood that intermediate bodies of all types are undergoing unprecedented changes under the pressure of social networks. Now, to look at all the major categorical changes that current politics is undergoing, we must ask ourselves the following question: in the neopolitical world, what is truth?

First, we must say one thing to ourselves: we cannot escape our human nature. *Errare humanum est*, it is said! But the full sentence attributed to Seneca says: *errare humanum est, perseverare diabolicum*. Error is human, stubbornness in error is diabloic. It is normal to be wrong. It is dangerous to lock yourself in the bubble of your mistake. When we talk about fake news, post-truth and everything that goes with it, we agree that the danger we brandish as the most horrible scarecrow is not people's occasional mistakes, but their stable systems of actions built on these mistakes.

Let's start with the fake news. This term, which became famous after its appropriation by Donald Trump, who thus ensured its very effective promotion, actually includes two distinct phenomena.

First type fake news is deliberately false information, offered to the public after a conscious sorting. In this way, after separating the true from the false, the supplier deliberately proposes the selection that is used to misinform rather than inform. They can be called **fake news by deliberation**.

The second type concerns non-distinct information, where factual verification has not been done, leading to a set of statements whose veracity is unknown. These are **fakes news by omission**.

These two "versions" of fake news can coexist in a single media space or be offered to the public separately. There are many examples of this, and any research on the subject is full of those examples. I can only direct the reader to the most interesting of these studies, notably in the prestigious journal Science[24], and in the Journal of Experimental Political Science[25]. The main points to be drawn from these studies are:

- We don't really know how many fake news there are on the Internet and in the media
- It has been proven that fake news continue to influence people's opinions and choices even after being scrutinized and proven false
- In the case of fake news by deliberation, they are usually designed to achieve virality
- Social networks are an important, but not the main relay for the propagation of fake news

What was discussed in the previous chapter, this perception of the crisis, which may not really exist, creates a more than favorable ground for the distribution of fake news. The international "trust barometer", proposed by the communication consultancy firm Edelman, says that people all over the world are, in a way, "trusting the crisis". That is, they are inclined to believe the news that everything is going badly rather than the other way around. The studies, above all the large study previously cited by van Ham et al., say that they are, in substance, wrong. But the facts remain the facts, and now speculators from all

---

[24] *The Science of Fake News*. Lazer, David M. J.; et al. in *Science*, mars 2018.
[25] *Displacing Misinformation about Events: An Experimental Test of Causal Corrections*. Nyhan, Brendan; Reifler, Jason in *Journal of Experimental Political Science*, 2015

the social spectrum are running in the race to better exploit this misjudgment.

In addition, history knows many examples of a kind of "crisis stretching", when a local problem is presented not as a separate whole, but as a projection of the Great Global Crisis which, according to the manipulators, has as its origin in this or that conspiracy, this or that community, this or that evil character. I remember that, during the vote on the highly controversial immigration law in the French National Assembly, a parliamentary assistant told me: "it will only have an impact on perhaps four hundred people at most, but people see a huge crisis and we must, as good communicators, respond to it". It would be interesting to ask the question, why and following what experiences people believe that there is a real immigration crisis in France... And not only in France. Donald Trump's rhetoric on the state of emergency, the so-called disaster on the country's southern border, is precisely an instrumentalization of this evidence-resistant perception of crisis.

It is often in this type of context that observers describe the post-truth society. This term, the word of the year 2016 according to the very prestigious Oxford dictionary, is not new, however. Journalists are able to trace this word back to 1992, even though its use has increased by 2000% since then, according to the BBC's count. This word is often used as a commentary to Donald Trump's photos, but it could well have been used under Bill Clinton's photos, for example.

The political world has also seen developments in parallel with deindustrialization in business, aligned with the trend towards a "marketing society". In the United States, Bill Clinton initiated the transformation of politics into what was called "showbiz for uglies" - an inclusive spectacle presented in a series of national experiments. In the United Kingdom, this was illustrated by Tony Blair's role in his public reaction to Princess Diana's death. The extent to which these phenomena are better understood as myths than as a reality was well illustrated in Adam Curtis' recent film *HyperNormalization*.

At the turn of the century, the government was already talking less about the "truth" than about how a set of different "truths" could be constructed. The famous "spindoctors", the often-demonized communication advisors, took the spotlight. We came up with the idea of the PR government, with examples like the war in Iraq, as it is shown in another recent great movie, *Vice*. As we know today, the facts have taken a back seat.

Meanwhile, the art of governing was also absorbed by "evidence-based" managerialism, the largely exclusive process with which Hillary Clinton, for example, had been negatively associated in the 2016 elections.

The approach taken by Tony Blair during his term as British Prime Minister, by Barack Obama, and by their respective administrations, namely the subdivision of politics between cultural experience and technocratic management, has made a double contribution to the social construction of the "post-truth". The abovementioned Oxford dictionary defines it as follows:

A reference to or designation of circumstances in which objective facts are less influential in the construction of public opinion than appeals to emotions and personal beliefs.

Of course, a legitimate question arises: how often in the history of the political world have opinions been formed by rational arguments? It could even be argued that in Europe, for example, for centuries marked by the dominance of the Church in political affairs, the rational had little value. And that would be a valid argument. Yet, during that time, the people were not a source of legitimacy for the political class. Divine law is well named: there was no real two-way political and social relationship between kings and their administrations on the one hand, and the people on the other. Thus, rational truth did not matter in politics in the end. While today, the responsibility for choice lies with the people in most Western countries, and in some ways, even in countries like Russia.

The Greeks understood this well. In Plato and Aristotle's Athens, and later in Roman society, rhetoric, persuasion, were phenomena understood and integrated into the "citizen education". The power that others can exercise over our choices, even our values, was both respected and feared, but blind acceptance was not really welcome. While today, what replaces the rhetoric - the

neopolitics

manipulation, the advertising, the big data we talked about etc. - is not the same as the rhetoric. - is not really "noble". Conviction no longer involves, as the definition proposed above states, facts, but personal emotions and beliefs.

Philosophically speaking, this is not new. For almost half a century now, it has been said that there is no position outside our own particularities to establish universal truth. It was one of the key principles of postmodernism, a concept that emerged in the 1980s after the publication of Jean-François Lyotard's *La condition postmoderne*. In this respect, since we are "postmodern", we have prepared the ground for an era of "post-truth". Or, as I prefer to say - not only because of the coherence with the title of this book, but also and above all because of the fact that the truth has not disappeared to leave us a world *after* it, - of "neotruth", of new, modified truth that is, just like neopolitics, largely elusive.

Neotruth is based on two pillars: the **right to opinion** and **trust**. The law justifies that this or that thing has the right be said, launched into public debate. Trust, in the societal sense, allows us to use things stated by others as true without immediate empirical confirmation. Both are extremely important, crucial, in the neopolitical functioning.

The right to an opinion comes from one of the two sources. The first is the legal source, for example the Constitution, which guarantees freedom of speech. It creates a framework for neo-truth, because it allows the expression of all kinds of information, such as, for example, "vaccines lead to autism", or "there is a migrant crisis in our country". The particularity of this pseudo-legitimacy is that it is, in fact, indisputable, although the justification of a statement by the right to bring it out into the open is a bit pulled by the ears. The second source of the right to opinion is evidence. They also provide the right to have this or that opinion - but also require intellectual defense, often active.

In most cases, the bearers of neotruth appeal to personal beliefs, which have no evidence-generated right to exist, but have the one generated by the legislative texts in force. In this way, there is no call to truth, and the justification for the fact does not lie in empirical evidence, but in the text defining the framework for the expression of opinion. "I believe it and I say it because I have the corresponding right, and you must listen to me and follow me." A new dangerous discursive practice, but one whose mastery is unfortunately necessary in the current context.

The New Zealand researcher Robert Nola proposes the following diagram to "map" the structure of beliefs:

neopolitics

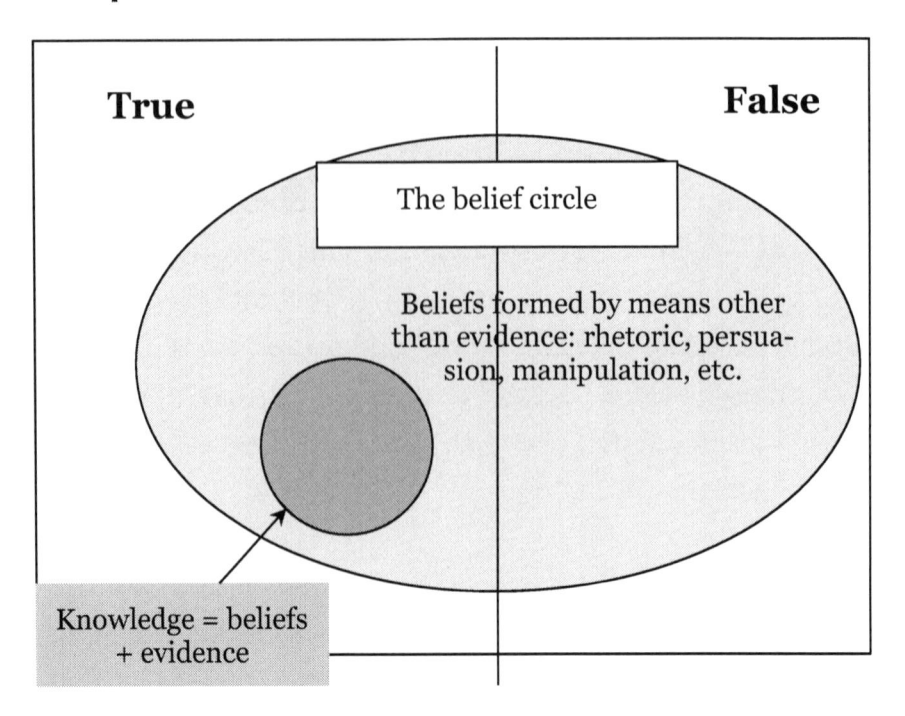

```
         True                              False

              ┌─────────────────────┐
              │  The belief circle  │
              └─────────────────────┘

                 Beliefs formed by means other
                 than evidence: rhetoric, persua-
                 sion, manipulation, etc.


   Knowledge = beliefs
       + evidence
```

We see here that in the whole universe of facts, true and false, there is what Nola calls the circle of beliefs, that is the complete display of facts that constitute the vision of the person's world. For this person, there is no difference between true information and false information, as long as he or she is convinced of its veracity either through evidence (in which case we can talk about *knowledge*) or through other means, such as rhetoric, persuasion, publicity, or different types of manipulation. Let us repeat that for the person, as long as he or she does not have direct access to evidence, not all "belief" constitutes knowledge, and therefore the veracity or otherwise of this or that statement belonging to that field does not really matter in his or her perception.

igor lys

A very simple example illustrates this phenomenon. Let's take one of the most famous astronomical facts: that the Earth revolves around the sun. We *know that*, but in our immediate experience, we cannot *prove* it. This, for millennia, organized universal belief in the world was that was not heliocentric.

But how then can we explain this certainty that we all have when we say that it is indeed the Earth that revolves around the sun and not the other way around? And what does this have to do with neopolitics?

So, we arrive at something crucial in the new relationship to the facts, born with the societal changes we are talking about on these pages. Paul Faulkner, the professor of philosophy at the British University of Sheffield, calls this something, "knowledge from trust". This particular type of belief, quite distinct from knowledge from evidence, allows us to have the same certainty as if we had direct evidence and testimonies about the fact in question. Knowledge by evidence is, undoubtedly, one of the great successes of human society, a *sine qua none* condition for progress. It would be impossible, without it, to advance science, but also to ensure governance, to conduct business. To ensure the proper functioning of this very important means of transmission, a number of markers have been created. Signs of quality" of information, references that remove, in theory, the need to look for evidence of a particular belief ourselves, as long as these markers are present on the information we are given. Of course, there have always been many abuses on this point. But in the neotruth, in the era of neopolitical changes, these abuses become so easy to replicate, markers become so vulnerable to counterfeiting, that the whole knowledge system of trust appears broken. Just look at the number of people who believe that the Earth is flat!

Everyone, without exception, needs sources of trust. We used to know that journalists were one of them, or maybe the evening paper's editorial, or our parents, our mentors, our personal gurus. Secret services, private detectives, the police, philosophers and scientists, all could be our sources. But with the Internet, they are all affected by the very tough competition which is the unlimited supply of information. Look again at Robert Nola's scheme: the circle of beliefs is large, and today the media, journalists, fake scientists and brokers of speculation of all kinds provide you with lots and lots of new truths in which we want to believe, because we are trained to base our actions on the knowledge acquired through trust.

The public trusts very easily. It believes that everything that the "experts" say on TV sets or on Facebook groups is knowledge by evidence, evidence that those experts had had directly and that they transmit through public channels. The public also believes that experts provide them with all the information at their disposal. It believes that the scale of communication, i.e. the strength of distribution, is proof of truthfulness. While:

- the experts may serve unknown agendas and communicate only part of the information;
- the scale of information distribution can be purchased like any other product;
- experts do not necessarily hold their knowledge, which may very well be included in their own circle of beliefs, from evidence.

I used the term "public", but the "elite" decision-makers are just as likely to have this easy trust weakness. Examples of pure and hard manipulation, such as the famous Powell vial that justified the war in Iraq, convey a somewhat diabolical view of the manipulative elites. But they are just as able not to see the truth. The example mentioned in one of the previous chapters, the Mubarak "inductivist turkey", is just a drop in the ocean of facts that confirm it. Of course, the elites have more resources to produce these fake news and use the community of opinion relays to ensure this fake knowledge through trust settles with the public. But as with the crisis of intermediate bodies, the equivalence of speech mentioned above means that manipulation can now operate in both directions. Sometimes, a moving photo on social networks is all it takes for governments to react violently even before the veracity of the photo is confirmed.

As the famous Soviet and later Russian linguist Andrei Zalizniak said in his speech at the 2007 Solzhenitsyn Prize reception:

neopolitics

"Yes, there are aspects of the world order where the truth is hidden and, perhaps, inaccessible. Yes, there are cases where a layman is right, and all the professionals are wrong. But the main change [in the perception of truth] is that these situations are not perceived as rare and exceptional as they really are, but rather as universal and ordinary.

And their psychological profitability is a huge incentive to accept and believe them. If all opinions have the same value, if they are equal, I can sit down and send my opinion immediately on the Internet, without complicating my task with years of study or with the acquisition of knowledge about what is already known on this subject by those who have devoted many years of research.

This psychological profitability exists for the writer who writes that, but also to an important degree, for the reader: a sensational refutation of what was considered yesterday a truth, frees him from the feeling of his own lack of education, places him all at once above those who have studied the corresponding traditional wisdom, which, as he has now learned, is worth nothing"

Cases like this are known and can be seen at the highest levels of state.

As a result, with the results we know, fake news of this type undermine trust in this proxy knowledge at all levels. The major media, from Le *Monde* to *New York Times*, are launching their fact-checking services, which are only the means to try to restore this trust. But the doubt is already there. Even the indicators that used to speak, such as the absence of negative information balances, are no longer sufficient. Scandals, such as the Séralini Affair named after the French researcher who "proved" that the consumption of genetically modified corn leads directly to cancer, generate clouds even above scientific publications, the last bastion of trust. The antivaxxers movements, which go so far as to affirm that vaccines are one of the causes of autism, prove that in the digital world there are no longer any universal references, no wells of knowledge from which everyone, without exception, could draw the reliable knowledge by trust.

In politics, and especially in current neopolitics, this series of phenomena plays one of the main roles. Actors like Nigel Farage, the eminent fighter against the European Union, one of the fiercest promoters of Brexit - disappeared from circulation shortly after the victory of his cause - can say a lot about that, he who had sprinkled the British with slogans as false as they were convincing ("We send 350 million pounds to the EU every week, let us instead finance our public health system!"). The new relationship to facts, unprecedented in the history of human thought, creates an unprecedented situation where

neopolitics

the public resigns itself, in a way, to supporting a cause despite the absolute absence of direct evidence, or even in the presence of a competing evidence. Let us take the example of the Trump Wall. When the sultry American president talks about an invasion, and the liberal media show, with the supporting facts, that there is no invasion, the two accuse each other of manipulating opinions, and each group remains with its beliefs, making that the sources for the arguments are not at all in the field of verifiable facts. While these very facts are more accessible than ever!

We are filled with knowledge by trust, but surprisingly, we do not really want to verify the sources of that trust. The zone of intellectual comfort now prevails over the zone of truth. Global warming, perhaps the most important phenomenon of our time by its magnitude, is an interesting case, because knowledge by trust would be almost contradictory with knowledge by evidence for many people. And many very powerful people use this apparent contradiction to push their short-term, profit-driven agendas.

With their right to opinion and beliefs drawn from non-verifiable sources, the hundreds of millions of voters (and therefore sources of legitimacy) in the world represent a *potential pool of power*, which candidates on all sides consider as a pure dehumanized reserve. Their relationship to the facts makes them little more than resources, a pool of political energy that can be used with well-delivered neotruths. On the one hand, by distributing fake news by deliberation, and on the other hand, by neutralizing people's sensitivity to fake news by omission.

This ultra-technocratic approach does not work in the long term. We saw this with Emmanuel Macron, who received in his face the need for political balance represented by the yellow vests, with Trump, even with Vladimir Putin. We will undoubtfully see it with Jair Bolsonaro and Ukrainian President Poroshenko. But how can we compete with these merchants of truths? Through a coherent, technical but human approach. The neopolitical approach.

In the next chapters, I will give an overview of some of the tools we can use, already today, to transform the potential power of sources of legitimacy into real power, while maintaining respect for the human side of those who, unfortunately, do not want a true truth.

neopolitics

Part 2. Neopolitical marketing

It would be pointless to talk about neopolitics if it did not provide any concrete solutions, did not provide any tangible instruments for acquiring power, governance and analysis in the world described, albeit quite briefly, on the previous pages. The very essence of all the intellectual work that separates neopolitics from politics, the reason for the very creation of this "label" that helps us to distinguish changes in the way this "thing of the polis" is done, - this essence consists in developing tools that would allow us to exploit what intellectual speculation can identify as new trends, as openings.

We are used to talking, when we talk about the practical side of power (some people talk about "applied power"), about political marketing. However, its very concept is, if you think about it, quite strange. As we will see below, the gurus of "classic" marketing, first and foremost Philip Kotler, have tried to prove that "selling" a candidate is not very different from selling a chocolate bar. An entire generation of specialists, from Washington to Beijing, has been raised in this approach. The notable difference is Russia where, at the beginning of the Yeltsin era, the profession of political communication advisor, arrived in social reality *before* the commercial mindset and the commercial structures themselves appeared. Since then, in the countries of the former USSR, these specialists have been called *polittechnologi*, or "political technologists", following the term coined by one of the first of them, Grigory Kazankov. This name is very interesting, because it reflects a reality that Western specialists often pretend to ignore: politics is not really a "market", and, however sensitive it may be to social engineering, working in it cannot be summed up either in the aspect of "sales" (supposed in the concept of marketing), or in the simple management of information (implied by the work of a "communicator"). Sensitive to highly volatile variables, any political equation contains social (including social feedback), cultural and economic components, and above all, politics implies a level of responsibility that is rarely achieved in the private sector. Thus, the work of those who advise political actors, whether in an election or in ongoing action, will always be different in scope from that of "classic" marketers.

As Heather Savigny of the University of Birmingham points out[26], political marketing relies on "ordinary" marketing assumptions to describe political behavior. These assumptions are explicitly based on neoclassical economic statements about behavior. In political science, these hypotheses are used by orthodox rational choice theory - rational choice provides a series of analytical models for inferring ontological implications and making predictions. But in the neopolitical world, where models of this kind clash with irrational reality amplified by ubiquitous technology, neopolitical marketing must deal with an unprecedented situation. In fact, it should stop being political *marketing* to become more that political *technology* or, to be even more precise, *strategic political technology* - to remain true to the name introduced on the very cover of this *neopolitical* book. This strategic technology can be defined as follows:

The techniques, know-how and instruments that can be used to acquire / maintain power.

I am convinced that these instruments must, above all, respond to the three main challenges identified at the beginning of this book: total competition, the crisis of personal brands, and media permanence. On the following pages, I will give an overview of some of these techniques, both to arouse the curiosity of specialists, and to give the

---

[26] In *Journal of Political Marketing*, vol. 3 — 1 of 2003, page 21

general public an opportunity to better understand the political communication to which it is subject.

I will start with the neopolitical personal brands that are, for me, the basis of all communication. Far from the American style *branding* vision, i.e. the coding of certain types of messages in the visual and textual aspects of the given brand, my approach inherits more from Thomas Gad than from Kotler. It is based not on the *attribution of the* brand *to* a person (or a party) following the research, but rather on the *extraction of the* brand *from* the person (or the decision-makers of the party) using specific techniques. These techniques also allow a kind of "reverse-engineering" of political communication, important in the world where the public must have at its disposal powerful decoding instruments, in order to protect itself from fake news of all kinds.

Then I will talk about how this brand, built around a specific matrix, can be translated into a flexible and effective communication strategy adapted to any kind of rivalry, whether with colleagues in the political world, or with commercial brands or digital stars.

And to conclude this book, I will address the question of how, in my opinion, time should be managed in political decision-making and the subsequent communication. When I talk about decision-making, I obviously do not forget reaction communication or response communication, but the decision to communicate a particular message at a particular time remains at the heart of the problem.

neopolitics

As I said above, my two objectives here are to arouse the curiosity of the specialists with whom I will be happy to discuss the different practical aspects of the techniques described, and to help all commentators on political action, whatever their degree of involvement in this, say, "industry", to analyze them. The reduction of the passionate and emotional side in the political discussion, and therefore in decision-making (on both sides of the barricades), is at the heart of the process.

igor lys

Political brands

The brand is one of the pillars of marketing. The cornerstone of any communication, the brand's religion has its many gods and apostles - from Philip Kotler to David Scott, the list is long. Those who have worked, even for a single day, in any election, know how much the positioning of the candidate or party nowdays depends on these *brandbooks* written for a fortune.

Francesc Dominguez, from the political marketing consulting firm Barton Consultants, describes it wonderfully:

> *"The main strategy in political life… is the ability to develop our main strengths or virtues, which distinguishes us from others and which society values. To increase our chances of success, we need to know what we want and what we don't*

want, and develop a clear plan or roadmap to get there."

This roadmap is precisely the brand. And now one of the biggest questions in political marketing is emerging before us: is the political brand a brand like any other?

Jacques Séguéla, a French political marketing guru with about twenty campaigns (and almost as many victories) to his credit, explained in 2011, in an interview with the magazine *l'ADN*, that there is a great fundamental difference: "Political marketing, he said, is the marketing of the offer... The marketing of consumer products is more like the marketing of the demand... On the one hand, there is the choice, on the other hand, there is the manufacture of the desire. Political advertising is by far the most democratic." Interestingly, Kotler, who we like to consider as the founding father of marketing (and whom Séguéla had surely read) had already made, as early as 1975, a kind of answer in advance[27] to all those who sought to explain the difference between political and commercial marketing by this type of generalities. He explained that in fact, if the difference between the two there is, it is not where you are looking for it at all. Séguéla's argument was, thirty-six years before it was formulated, denied by the master himself. It would be useful here to display some of Kotler's arguments, because without

---

[27] Cf. *Overview of Political Candidate Marketing*. Philip Kotler in *NA - Advances in Consumer Research Volume 02*, édition Mary Jane Schlinger, Ann Abor, MI, 1975, pages de 761 à 770

understanding these sometimes non-obvious similarities, it is impossible to explain the differences - essential for the design of appropriate tools.

- **"Any specific commercial product, such as a can of beans or a ton of steel, has relatively fixed characteristics at any given time. The political candidate, on the other hand, is more variable. And in addition, the political candidate can respond.** That is true, but the variable nature of the political product is very similar to that of *services* in the commercial world. Services are inseparable from the people who provide them. A hairdresser, for example, can respond, which changes the quality of his services, etc.
- **"Classic" products are normally available for purchase at any time, at the discretion of the buyer. While political products are only "put on sale" every few years"**. Kotler's objection here is that there are examples of economic products that buyers can only acquire at certain times. "You can only buy a Rembrandt when it is put up for sale or auction," says Kotler. Similarly, you can only enroll in a college during certain periods of the year. Many government contracts have advertised tender dates. The frequency of purchases therefore makes it impossible to distinguish between commercial and non-commercial

products - even more so since in the neopolitical world, permanent competition almost eliminates this notion of regularity. Certainly, in professional language, *political communication* replaces *political marketing* precisely because of this new relationship with the media, but it is only a change of facade. Basically, and we will come back to this later, it is only a question of extending campaign practices to the entire duration of a mandate.

- **"The buyer of a commercial product or service generally expects direct and personal benefits within a reasonable period of time. Many voters do not expect to benefit from this type of advantage from their voting record**. Yet there are a variety of commercial products and services that do not appear to provide any personal or short-term benefits, and that people still buy, such as insurance. People also contribute to various charitable causes for which they do not receive personal benefits. On the other hand, many voters are quite active in some campaigns and act as if they anticipate such personal benefits. The charismatic candidate can also give a large number of voters the feeling that they will personally benefit from his or her election.
- **"The objectives and means of a merchant and a political candidate are different. The merchant is looking for profit. The political candidate is looking for power. The**

company is trying to get more profits by creating satisfied customers. The political candidate is not so clearly seeking more power by creating satisfied citizens. In reality, companies pursue multiple objectives, as do political candidates. In fact, there are commercial companies seeking power, and political candidates seeking profit. In addition, companies and political candidates can choose from a range of philosophies on which to base their marketing. There are politicians who aim to produce satisfied citizens; and companies who aim for quick profits.

It can be seen that the elements cited allow political marketers to use a wide range of means and tools developed for commercial products, drawing both inspiration and techniques from the stacks of different commercial sectors. But the fact remains that most of these tools, and in particular the brand we are talking about here, sometimes need to be updated. This is especially true when it comes to meeting very specific political demands that have little or no equivalence in the business world. These major differences belong to the three main areas: relations with the traditional media, the different philosophy of "buying", and the concept of "brand bearers" which is very different in politics.

One of the main differences between neopolitical marketing (i.e. the acquisition and exercise of power in

neopolitics

the neopolitical world, where the very architecture of this power is constantly changing and is based on unprecedented technological achievements that themselves evolve on a daily basis) and classical marketing lies in the fact that the political world is, *par excellence*, a world of adversity and combat. Unlike commercial products and services, political action, whatever its media positioning, is not based on a one-off act (such as consuming a product, or putting on a perfume, or developing a website, etc.), nor on a series of acts united by a contract (such as insurance, close protection, childcare, etc.). Political action is a *valuable action*, the framework of which is defined only by a system of responses to different signals. The fact of "buying" a politician, i.e. contributing to his or her ascension or retention in power through voting or other membership, in return offers only very few certainties of action. As policies evolve in a context, it is their decision-making system in that context that defines and differentiates them from each other, more than legislative proposals and other ad hoc acts. It is a struggle since there are camps each of which pursue their own objective. From an ordinary observer's point of view, these are often the general left-right, or liberal-conservative (depending on the country) divisions, , and the particular flag bearers of a particular camp, whether men and women or parties, are then chosen according to their programmes and the emotional attraction they generate.

Let us take the example of sport. As American researcher Amy Chua, who has devoted a number of studies to the issue of political tribalism, says, there is something political about the support supporters give to their football or baseball teams. They belong to a group, the one of their team, often united also by their geographical location (but not always, one of the challenges of the big clubs being precisely to seek the expansion of their fan bases to other cities, countries or continents). Fans discuss strategies, recruits, and pay to attend matches (both virtually, via pay TV, and in real life, in the stadiums). What happens during the matches is the *proxy competition*, i.e. a confrontation whose victory belongs to all the supporters, when the physical effort necessary to reach it is only made by a group specifically designed for this purpose.

Of course, the parallels with politics are not direct. The group - in a way, an intermediate body - is not really elected, but rather constituted by a kind of technocratic power. The rules of the game are predefined, and both teams have the same clear objective, success or failure being, in sport, simple and very well described categories. We can make a very long list of the differences between the two areas, but what interests us here is the concept of a "power of attorney" that they share. In politics, the race to power and its exercise requires that sources of legitimacy (the people in most Western democracies, the financial elite too, but in some cases, it is the army, or the religious body...) transmit and maintain a kind of power of attorney, a procuration, for political struggle. They support some causes and fight others, but except for a few extreme cases, they are only "fans" in this battle, leaving the instruments of the struggle - legitimate violence, legislation, regulations and controls - in the hands of a "team". For this team and its "players" to be able to convince the bearers of legitimacy to ensure this projection of power, they must propose a clear and unequivocal formulation of what they are *for* and what they are *against*. Then, whatever the target audience (voters in a national or local vote, but also perhaps key donors or, for example, in the context of an appointment validated by Parliament, the members of that Parliament), it is necessary to build a communication campaign based on a series of messages most likely to shift the choice of decision-makers in the "correct" direction. It is precisely the architecture and conduct of such campaigns that political, and therefore neopolitical, technologies seek to perfect.

The brand plays one of the most important roles, if not the crucial one. It defines what must be delivered to the targeted audiences, and what, once it has penetrated the mind of that audience, must develop into a system of meaning that will guide the choice to give the power of attorney to this or that person, to this or that party.

To be effective, the brand must ensure the three key elements:
1. *Trust*: the candidate (individual or institutional) must be perceived as a trustworthy close friend;
2. *Clarity*: the candidate's value proposition must be articulated, understandable to its audience, unambiguous, and transposable into different communication formats;

3. *Coherence*: it must be in intellectual harmony with the social, political and economic context. The political brand that is not coherent and does not meet the real needs of the context, becomes a speculative political brand – a dangerous thing to happen.

neopolitics

The Neopolitical Brand Matrix

In the context of neopolitical marketing, or neopolitical strategy in general, I propose an instrument that I call the NBM, for *neopolitical brand map*. The NBM is a result of work and reflection based on the thoughts of my branding mentor, Thomas Gad, who unfortunately died in 2017, stated for the most of them in his book "4D branding" prefaced by Sir Richard Branson. With the contribution of my professional experience, and the work of my colleagues such as Carsten Claus of the German company Oberkorn, author of many political and commercial brands in Germany, I propose a matrix that is both practical for a political actor and useful for the general public. It allows the definition of all the key elements of a communication strategy, and does so by taking into account the neopolitical (i.e. - political with new challenges) aspect of the world it will evolve in.

Thomas Gad had theorized already at the end of the 1990s the transition from "transactional" brands, the fruits of industrial society, to "relational" brands whose importance has only increased with the Internet. In the 2010's, we move on to the so-called "user experience" brands, whose main components are the retention of attention, the elements of surprise, and the duration of brand consumption - relational brands only exist in the consumer's mental space at the time of consumption and need (or even craving), but the emotions associated with them are the same. User experience brands, on the other hand, tend to exist by constantly reinventing themselves. The best examples are applications for smartphones which, by offering more or less the same service, are constantly improving their interface and functionalities with regular updates.

Political actors must become these user experience brands. When transactions (for example, voting) are there, when the relationship is established (for example, through instant reactions on social networks), we enter the world of permanent and merciless neopolitical competition, and it is the constant improvement of the support experience that becomes the core of the problem.

As Gad reminds us, our brains are designed to consciously take information and transform it into

neopolitics

unconscious experiences[28]. It's like driving a car: first you learn to do it consciously and then you "know" how to do it automatically. Thus, some studies (Hawkins, Dijkstehuis...) say that it is the unconscious that is responsible for the choices we make, the consciousness being simply unable to show the same computing power. The conscious mind would also make better decisions when the choice is limited to a few options, and with few variables at stake. When it comes to complex things, the unconscious is faster and more efficient.

Brands are intellectual constructs that transform conscious learning about a product, a person or an organization into an unconscious perception, a kind of perceptual "package". The neopolitical brand matrix is a tool that allows you to do this in an almost playful way.

Given what has been said above, the NBM is different from a trademark matrix in its "for and against" aspect. The particularity of political brands, as we saw earlier, lies in this strong duality. We support a political actor because he or she is fighting for something, and at the same time, against something. We support a *way of fighting*. That is why the proposed matrix contains this unique component, this combination of positive and negative, expressed in the matrix by symbols (+) and (-).

The NBM matrix is as follows:

---

[28]Thomas Gad. *Customer Experience Branding: Driving Engagement Through Surprise and Innovation,* Kogan Pages Publishers, 2016. Page 32.

	(+)	(-)
Substance	Who (or what) is the candidate?	
Mission Statement	In the candidate's ideal world, what cause is being realized?	In the candidate's ideal world, what cause is excluded from society?
Value proposition	What is the real utility of the candidate? What concrete proposals does he or she (or it) make?	
Methodology	How will the candidate achieve his or her objectives and value proposition?	How will the candidate block unacceptable initiatives, hinder the progress of his political opponents?
Positioning	What differentiates the candidate from other representatives of his or her own political family?	What differentiates the candidate from his competitors representing other political currents?
Values	What are the keywords that make the candidate worthy of a friendly trust?	What values are absent in the candidate's ideal world?
Vision	In what social and political context does the candidate see himself in the future?	What problems, what phenomena present today are absent in the candidate's ideal world in the future?
Style	What characterizes the candidate's style?	
Political Slogan	Which sentence summarizes this matrix?	

neopolitics

It should be noted that the word "candidate" may refer here to a person as well as to a political party or a civil movement. Candidacy is a general term, which does not necessarily refer to an election. One can be a "candidate for continued power" or a "candidate for leadership of the opposition".

Let's explain in detail the different parts of the matrix that makes up the Map.

Substance

This is about *what* and *who* the candidate *is*. This part of the Map is especially useful in the creation of the synthesis, which will be discussed below. But it allows us to give the dynamics of understanding to the rest of the picture.

The Substance can be formulated in a thousand ways, but I always prefer a simple formula: the explanation of the nature of the candidate, the direct and clear statement, accompanied by a single adjective, and not related to the other elements of the matrix. For example, "young man", or "famous political party", but not "honest woman" or "visionary association". The quality of the candidate is explained and developed in the other boxes which, in the best of cases, are filled in during long and deep working sessions. The purpose of the Substance is to indicate the most basic facts, to explain to the public with whom they are dealing.

For a complete example, let us imagine a candidate named Jean-François Example, who wants to become mayor of Imaginetown and its ten thousand inhabitants. Quite conservative, he likes to put forward his family father side, so here's how we define him:

Proud father and husband, born and raised in Imaginetown

neopolitics

Mission Statement

The mission of a brand, political or not, is, in the words of Carsten Claus of the consulting firm Oberkorn, the "bold why". An objective, an important yet clear task, which consists in following/supporting the brand's great "practical" vision. For example, one could say that Kylian Mbappé's great vision is to be France's top scorer against Germany. Then the mission would be: "to give all young children a perspective to which hard work can lead", and the method, to which we will return: "to develop a game that the Germans will only understand after I have scored".

The mission aims to establish a relationship of trust with the target audience. It responds to a need for emotional attachment to a cause and ensures that the governmental "power of attorney" is consistent with the society's vision of the source of legitimacy that is targeted by political marketing. Its main characteristic is that the mission is not linked to the current political context. It must not change from one election to another, from one party convention to another. While, depending on the candidate's successes and responsibilities (individual or those of a party, regardless), the elements of the NBM such as the value proposition can evolve, the mission remains at the heart of the brand's foundation. It is a civic mission, more than a political one, and it must not possess an internal dynamic. It is preferable that the candidate (or the party leaders, if any) define it himself.

The (+) side of the mission is defined by the cause at the heart of the fight: what is the candidate fighting for? What society, what world would be for him such that he could, like Dr. Faust, say "stop, stop, you're so beautiful, oh moment"?

This wording must be precise and direct, but not for a quantifiable purpose. The mission (+) must include a dream aspect, which would make you want to participate in. Like for example:

Building a fairer country, including fewer inequalities between rich and poor, men and women

For Jean-François Example, it will be -

Make the people of Imaginetown happy and proud of their town

In its (-) side, the mission refers to the opposing ideology, the cause to be fought, the enemy to not let advance. Then candidate for the presidency of the French Republic, François Hollande said, during a meeting, that his enemy was "finance". Not necessarily consistent with its real policy (which is a real brand issue), this micro-slogan had positioned Hollande as a "anti-financial" values mission carrier.

Examples of missions (-):

neopolitics

Combat the ultraliberal drift and any attempt to weaken French social protection

Do not let anyone, neither man nor party, touch the freedoms guaranteed by the first two amendments to the American Constitution

Do everything legally possible not to give even an ounce of power to those who advocate collaboration with the West at the expense of Russia's national interests

Our imaginary candidate, on the other hand, proposes this as his mission (-):

Do not let political, social or other divisions influence the pride and happiness of Imaginetown residents

Value proposition

This is the "product" that the candidate offers to his public. If the mission allows sources of legitimacy to identify themselves with the candidate and thus justify their power of attorney, the value proposition gives the rational reasons. These are the concrete measures, flagship measures, that the candidate carries in his programme. You can't have more than three.

The value proposition answers the main question of any voter or influencer: how useful is my choice for me? What tangible result can I achieve by interacting with the brand - including voting? But also by supporting it publicly, on social networks, or even in private conversations.

The value proposition can evolve over time, but must always remain in line with the mission and method, which are preferably immutable. Because nothing is worse than inconsistency in communication and political action. Do not follow the example of Manuel Valls, former French Prime Minister elected as a Member of Parliament on the slogan "Toujours avec vous" and the campaign built in this direction. Then to leave to run for mayor of Barcelona.

The value proposition talks about concrete and immediately achievable measures, if of course the candidate is elected or supported. The laws to be passed, the measures to be taken, the proposals for decrees, are among them. Jean-François Exemple, after long working sessions with his communication advisors, decides to define it as follows:

Pride in the beautification of the entire city, and the best public services in the department. Happiness through economic growth ensured by measures for small traders. Unity through constant communication with citizens through a digital debate platform, and the taking of decisions validated by the population

neopolitics

Methodology

This is the great "how". How will our candidate carry out his program? How does he plan to do that? And how will he counter opposing initiatives? All candidates will be judged by sources of legitimacy in relation to their ability to implement the program. For example, if the pro-Brexit campaign were to present the neopolitical brand matrix - or if voters had ventured to fill it out for it - the methodological gap would have raised serious questions. Same for Trump, same for everyone. It is crucial to know how to formulate your method in a few short and understandable sentences, and above all, to then *do* according to the stated vision.

Thus, for Jean-François Example, the matrix at this level would be filled in as follows:

Method (+) :

Establish a digital platform for debate on all future major decisions of the city hall, and take these decisions only after they have been discussed and validated by the city's residents

An established political party could define its method simply as a continuation of the work done over the years.

Method (-) :

Organize a committee of experts to be consulted following any conflict involving the unity of the city's inhabitants

If you want to fill out the Neopolitical Brand Map to better understand this or that candidate, and you have trouble defining his method, what is a real problem. And if you are this same candidate, and you are setting up a political branding process, be very careful to formulate your *modus operandi* correctly.

Positioning

We often hear, whatever the country, the different versions of the dubious statement "all rotten". All policies would be the same, and incidentally controlled by the "deep state", i.e. the richest oligarchs, none of whom escape any molecule of power. But this statement is false, and dangerous. All may be rotten, but certainly not in the same way! And the difference between the different candidates is precisely what tilts the balance. Of course, the mission, the method etc., including the difference. But it is the positioning that allows you to have a quick, precise and effective answer to the question that is so often asked, if only implicitly: what makes you different from others?

neopolitics

This is especially important if it is an internal competition within the same political family. When the actual political differences are minimal, how can we motivate the vote or other support?

For candidates with unclear positioning, there is always the risk of being targeted on this, as Emmanuel Macron was during his campaign.

Jean-François Exemple is the only candidate in his political family competing in Imaginetown who grew up in the city. The only one who has been both entrepreneur and elected in his hometown, he is the only one who is the true mayor-citizen

He is the only one who really thinks about people and their problems, and the only one who proposes listening solutions that go far beyond grievances, and that will accompany his work as mayor throughout the mandate.

Values

As we have said: trust is one of the pillars of the brand. More than that: as we have seen in the chapter dedicated to fake news, trust makes it possible to communicate a certain type of knowledge and, in extreme cases, it replaces the need for proof. This dangerous process is crucial in political combat, however, where opponents can emerge from embarrassing facts, or controversial polemics where trust in the candidate's speech may cost him victory or retention in power. It is precisely this trust that allows Vladimir Putin, for example, to promote a media agenda within his country that is out of step with the evidence provided by objective analysis. The same is true in Recep Erdogan's Turkey. But also in small towns in Algeria.

Trust had also enabled people not to be blinded by attacks on "their" party or candidate. Trust allows you to win, and to resist temptations. And it is generated by values. This list should only be said rarely, but all the rest of the communication, whether it takes place during a political meeting or a press interview, should support it. But be careful: a candidate's values must be his real values, or at least he must be sure that he can pretend to have full respect for them. If the Neopolitical Brand Map, drawn up with the candidate, stipulates that among his values is "honesty", but he has been indicted three times for embezzlement of public funds, there is a problem.

As for Mr. Example, his values (+) are:

Audacity, respect, listening, transparency, patriotism

As for the values (-), here, as in the other boxes, they are the elements to be fought, the defined and precise opponents. We should not be surprised to see something here that seems harmless to us. In the extremely cynical political debate, any value can become that of the enemy. And if, for example, corruption, greed and selfishness

neopolitics

seem almost natural to us like these hostile elements, so is egalitarianism for some, as well as freedom of speech!

Our dear Jean-François is fighting against:

Racism, hatred, selfishness, division

Vision

Let's imagine, the candidate won. The party has taken power. The President has all the support he needs. Which world are we heading into? What are the realities of the future for which the candidate is an ambassador? To properly define the vision, you have to ask yourself two questions: what will be in my ideal world in X years? And what is certainly not going to happen? And in this world, what will my place be?

Here is Mr. Example's answer. Vision(+) :

Jean-François Example will be able to make Imaginetown the locality of his region with the greatest satisfaction of the inhabitants of their town hall, and the highest rate of optimism in the region.

Vision(-) :

At the end of Mr. Example's term, the number of incidents related to hate and inequality will be among the lowest in the region

Style

The coherence of the brand also depends on its visual aspect. We are talking here about everything that is created by and for the candidate and that appeals to the eyes. From the website to the leaflets distributed at the markets, from how to dress with the party logo, from the decoration of its political meeting rooms to the design of its Twitter page. For someone, the style will be defined by words like "imperious, baroque, sophisticated, rich", while for the other, it will be "clear, refined, modern, simple"... Again, the style must correspond to the candidate. No one will understand if, for example, tomorrow Theresa May will start sneaking around, or on the contrary if the young opponent of Putin Alexei Navalny, who is very popular with young people in his country, will cover his website with virtual mouldings.

Jean-François Example is quite conservative, as we have already said, and therefore for him the style will be:

Classic, serious, calm, clear

Political Slogan

It is not just a campaign slogan, if at all. It is a general sentence that summarizes the entire Brand Map in a single statement. As "Connecting people" for the almost forgotten company Nokia, but also as "La Force tranquille" of Mitterrand.

The process of defining the brand policy slogan is a long one. It includes the work of communication experts, with the mandatory participation of the candidate (party leaders, if any). This slogan should, normally, survive a one-time campaign, and remain with the candidate in both digital and verbal media. Even if this tool is only very rarely used outside electoral unrest, we will see it more and more. Barack Obama wore his "Yes we can" for years. And more and more political brand owners will understand that these brands, with all their components including the slogan, must be worn over time. This will impact not only the perception, but also the political action itself, since it will have to see its coherence strengthened. If François Hollande had kept his "Change is now! "during the 5 years at the Elysée, he might have done some things differently? Who knows.

In any case, Jean-François Example worked well on his slogan, which he obviously wanted to be representative of his political brand map. Let's start by summarizing it:

| (+) | (-) |

igor lys

Substance	Jean-François Example, candidate for mayor of Imaginetown, father of a family born in the city	
Mission Statement	Make the people of Imaginetown happy and proud of their city	Do not let political, social or other divisions influence the pride and happiness of Imaginareville residents
Value proposition	Pride in the beautification of the entire city, and the best public services in the department. Happiness through economic growth ensured by measures for small traders. Unity through constant communication with citizens through a digital debate platform, and the taking of decisions validated by the population	
Methodology	Establish a digital platform for debate on all future major decisions of the city hall, and take these decisions only after they have been discussed and validated by the city's residents	Organize a committee of experts to be consulted following any conflict involving the unity of the city's inhabitants
Positioning	Jean-François Example is the only candidate in his political family competing in Imaginetown who grew up in the city. The only one who has been both entrepreneur and elected in his hometown, he is the only one who is the true mayor-citizen	He is the only one who really thinks about people and their problems, and the only one who proposes listening solutions that go far beyond grievances, and that will accompany his work as mayor throughout the mandate.
Values	Audacity, respect, listening, transparency, patriotism	Racism, hatred, selfishness, division
Vision	Jean-François Example will be able to make Imaginetown the locality of his region with the greatest satisfaction of the inhabitants of their town hall, and	At the end of Mr. Example's term, the number of incidents related to hate and inequality will be among the lowest in the region

neopolitics

	the highest rate of optimism in the region.	
Style	Classic, serious, calm, clear	
Political Slogan	Work hand in hand with you for the happiness of all of inhabitants of Imaginetown	

We can see that all the elements of the map are consistent with the mission, even appearing sometimes repetitive. This will not always be the case, but when it is, it is a good sign. This means that all the candidate's action, all communication revolves around his or her well-defined mission.

It should be noted that, in addition to the slogan, the Neopolitical Brand Map makes it possible to create a whole paragraph of synthesis and presentation. All you have to do is go to the websites of the various politicians and parties around the world to see how much more understandable even our imaginary little Jean-François can seem than they are. Let's compare, for example, its synthesis:

Jean-François Example, a father and a husband born and raised in Imaginetown, has the mission to make the people of his hometown happy and proud of where they live, and to protect that happiness and pride against political and social divisions. He will ensure this pride by beautifying the entire city, and organizing the best public services in his department, and this happiness by economic growth ensured by measures for small traders. It will combat dangerous divisions through constant communication with citizens through a platform for digital debate and decision-making validated by the public. Jean-François Example is the only candidate in his political family in Imaginetown who grew up in the town. The only one who was both an entrepreneur and an elected official in his hometown, he is the only one who is the true mayor-citizen. And, for all political families combined, he is the only one who really thinks about people and their problems, and the only one who proposes listening solutions that go far beyond grievances, and that will accompany his work as mayor throughout the mandate. Bold, respectful, always attentive and transparent in his actions, he fights racism, hatred, selfishness and division. Jean-François Example works to make Imaginetown the locality of his region with the greatest satisfaction of the inhabitants of their town hall, and the highest rate of optimism in the region.

...with the "Who are we" section of the La République en Marche site, Emmanuel Macron's political movement[29]. Here are the first paragraphs:

---

[29] https://en-marche.fr/le-mouvement

neopolitics

"There are more than 392,000 of us on the move all over France, from Lille to Bordeaux, from Paris to Marseille, Lyon, Strasbourg, from Sarthe to Vaucluse... Our movement is multiple, rich in your diversity and united around a common project.

It is a long way we are going together. A path that, day after day, moves the lines, breaks the partisan dichotomy that is now obsolete and calls on men and women of good will who are working together to build tomorrow's society. En Marche is the result of a collective reflection that puts citizens back at the heart of political life. Working today in tomorrow's world... That's Emmanuel Macron's bet!"

Which of the two presentations seems clearer, more complete to you?

The Neopolitical Brand Map is a very powerful tool that, like any brand, is at the heart of action and communication. The brand thus created will make it possible to establish a relationship of trust with the target audience, which will become the political capital necessary for any public action.

But also, this Map can and must serve this same public to better understand the positioning, often (in)voluntarily vague, of a given candidate. Analysing your speeches, messages posted on social networks, websites, and then trying to fill in the matrix proposed above, will help to find inconsistencies, to understand the real intentions.

In a world where populism attacks on all fronts, nothing is more important.

neopolitics

Permanent competition and the media 24 hours a day

How can we respond to the challenges of neopolitics? At the end of February 2019, French President Emmanuel Macron received the Swedish activist Greta Thumberg at the Elysée. At the age of 16, she mobilized all over Europe, and so she went to speak to President Macron in the same presidential palace that hosted John Kennedy or Muammar Gaddafi. If you still do not believe in neopolitics, give me an example in the history of such a welcome. The speech equivalence mentioned above creates the equivalent competition between the speech of a president and that of a student. Without Twitter, the activism of the brave Greta, who sat in front of the Swedish

Parliament for days and days to push it to act against global warming, would have been reduced to these few fine actions.

But the social networks, these multipliers of individual voice power, and the social dynamics mentioned in the chapter dedicated to intermediate bodies, are there. And just like this brave Swede, professional manipulators, Russian, Chinese and American trolls, commercial brands, comedians, youtubers and porn stars are, for better or for worse, in direct competition with any politician. And if today a certain respect for traditions imposes on us the vision that its two types of discourse do not have the same weight, tomorrow perhaps this will no longer be the case. Vladimir Putin does not have a Twitter account for the same reasons that lead him to refuse any electoral debate: he does not like competition.

And the one that politicians are beginning to live in the neopolitical media space is merciless. Brazilian MP Mamãe Falei said it in an interview in *Buzzfeed*, without ambiguity: "I guarantee that in Brazil, youtubers are more influential than politicians". The mechanisms of influence change in nature. Yesterday, young people imitated the codes of the great decision-makers to appear more convincing in their immediate social context. Today, major decision-makers are imitating the youth's codes to seek new sources of legitimacy. And tomorrow, who knows what will happen?

neopolitics

It is difficult to provide neutral and always effective tools for this type of competitive battle without context. Experience shows that these tools often need to be developed *ad hoc*, to fit a given set of objectives. However, we can give here some basics, some general notions about the *types of* tools that can be used in this kind of situation.

First of all, however, it must be understood that this permanent and total competition is very real. It is not an invention of agencies and consulting firms that want to capitalize, as they so often do, on their clients' fear of the unknown. I remember this dialogue with the right-hand man of a Republican American governor, where I was subjected to a rather violent criticism of my vision of things. Because, as this person told me, their election campaign targeted a very specific, well-managed audience that did not or hardly interact with the audience of network stars, "who are all[left-wing] Liberal assholes anyway"[30]. This view is understandable, but false. It is based on a lack of strategic vision. It is undeniable that in the context of an election campaign, it may seem appropriate to focus available resources on the defined target and, if it is not sensitive to a particular media, they could be ignored. This is even more true in the American campaigns, which are highly technical, including the division of electoral districts. But two things must be remembered: the

---

[30] A very American peculiarity, where bloggers of all types are often associated with the left, even though the accounts, true and false, pro-Trump which have ensured it almost absolute domination on social networks

first is that any campaign for one candidate is also a campaign against the others, and demotivating voters on the other side is sometimes more important than motivating their own; and the second is that if the campaign in question is successful, then we must start governing, that is, managing all audiences and not just the one who won. To do otherwise is a textbook case of dangerous political short-sightedness. Opponents will have already worked with opinion leaders, and for example new generations of voters will arrive with a mindset hostile to candidates who are not effective in competing with new web stars. The cases of large companies on Twitter, which are in dispute with Trump, also show this.

These two crucial points included, we can move on to the list of elements that constitute the basis of the competitive issue mentioned. Generic or *ad hoc* tools must first and foremost meet the challenges posed by this list:

1. **You must be prepared to respond to any type of comment from any type of social actor.** Before, it was not only possible, but normal and desirable to ignore messages of limited intellectual significance, or from actors far from any social influence (who, in any case, in 99% of cases did not even have the technical capacity to be heard). But when anyone can launch a petition that, however unmotivated, can reach hundreds of thousands of signatures; when anyone can create a Facebook event at first sight ridiculous but which

turns into a movement with national coverage; when any little alcoholic can record a video message to the president and which will be commented on by all my media (we have seen cases like this in Russia!) - then you have to be ready to answer it, and have solutions for any kind of solicitation;

2. **It is necessary to know how to ensure the** potentially automated **monitoring of** tomorrow's rising influencers and hot topics, for example Facebook events with a political connotation with the most important dynamic of growth in the number of participants;

3. **We must not be afraid to strike first** to neutralize potential dangerous subjects, and the harmful actors in the making. For this purpose, political structures use armies of digital supporters, often "trolls" (i.e. paid users who communicate only on selected topics, in a coordinated way and according to precise instructions). But sometimes you have to go up to the front line, not necessarily by naming your "target", but for example with proposals to neutralize any controversy before it really arises.

These three competitive challenges are linked to the extent that one stems from the other. On the detailed solutions to answer them, we could write about ten books like this one. As I said at the very beginning, the purpose here is to provide an overview of different types of approaches and tools.

The basis of all these tools is the *media strategy kit*. It is the document that governs technological and human solutions and the conditions for their implementation, as well as the corresponding protocols. Its objective - to transpose the Neopolitical Brand Map into the candidate's communication. Communication that we always liked to master, and that we no longer really master. We talk about media strategy because it is a roadmap for building cooperation, actions and reactions (including those of response) towards media of all types. And the word *kit* refers to the fact that these are prefabricated solutions that can, after some training, be used by any member of the candidate's team - much like aircraft cockpits, where once the pilot is trained to control a certain type of aircraft, he can do so at any time, regardless of the airline. This ease of use is necessary, since the media operate - as has been said more than once - around the clock. And in a world where slow response can be expensive, it is important that whoever is monitoring the networks can immediately provide the necessary response in the event of a serious or potentially serious situation. The absence of such a kit leads to what observers call amateurism. We in France know the phenomenon.

Perhaps the reasons for this lack of willingness to take these changes seriously lies in a sort of denial. Many people and institutions do not want to accept the

neopolitics

irreversibility of some of the changes in the way of doing things and living that have occurred over the past 20 years. We talked about it at the very beginning of this book: next to the cyclical changes, which are passing for a better return a few decades or a few centuries later, are the incredible changes, new, so fast that they become violent. And these changes, which give the "neo" to neopolitics, have come to stay.

We no longer wait to hear the latest news on a late TV news outlet at a specific time, or in the newspaper the next morning after the "big news" actually happened. Instead, the reports are broadcast on social media and news channels on a continuous basis, live as they occur. Journalists and editors struggle to be part of the news, and not fall behind - when it is the journalists who carry the news. Because if before the media consisted of traditional television, radio and print carriers, today their family has expanded to include many digital channels (including YouTube channels or Twitter accounts) where influencers are the spokespeople for current affairs rather than well-known and reputable journalists and anchors.

This era of social networks is the one in which creators and influencers have achieved online celebrity status by building a network of followers who trust what they have to say. We talked about it in the chapter on fake news. This follower network connects to watch videos and read blogs (or Facebook statuses...) regularly to get the latest news on a variety of topics, whether related to lifestyle, business, etc. - and of course, to politics, this queen of all topics. This is a new world of content that has many opinions and sometimes belongs to owners in a world where your target audience has instant access to information.

This change can be difficult, well, it *is,* but it also represents a huge opportunity for politics. It is on these opportunities that media strategy kits must be based. I will mention four of them[31], the most important ones.

Opportunity 1: more control over content

Thanks to new digital channels, politicians themselves can become influencers for their target audience - on this approach was built Bernie Sanders' campaign in 2016 and then Jean-Luc Mélenchon's in France in 2017, for example. A politician can become a true opinion leader by developing an excellent blog, or a political party brand can have a viral profile on social media, just by working hard on that. Interestingly, even if almost all political actors (at least in the West) say they understand this simple new media truth, very few take advantage of it, and often it is the representatives of extremes (extreme left with Mélenchon, extreme right with Trump or Viktor Orban or Jair Bolsonaro etc.). There are excellent opportunities to publish political brand content so that the focus will be on this famous targeted content strategy. Rather than hope that a media will repeat the story! It works

---

[31] This selection corresponds more or less to that made by the big data company Meltwater, which works a lot on the analysis of the dynamics of influence in the media world

very well for brands of all sizes, and it can also work for politics.

Alternatively, political structures can work directly with influencers on an individual basis to develop unique exclusivities that will resonate with their target audience. For example, in France, at the end of 2018, there was a joint project between the Ministry of Ecology and almost all the major youtubers in the country. The focus is on both quality (recognized content creators) and quantity (large audiences and high levels of responsiveness).

Opportunity 2: direct link with target audiences

Politicians, including institutions, can now either communicate directly with the public through their own channels or through influencers whose reach is already established. It is important to build trust through direct relationships when it comes to monitoring policy. If you can work with an influencer who has already established this trust through authentic communication, then you can exploit it. This is particularly interesting at the local level, where mayors, for example, can have new channels of direct contact with the population (e. g. through their Instagram accounts), and "raise" local influencers who will become their ambassadors among the target audiences

Perhaps tomorrow, press briefings at the White House or press briefings after the Council of Ministers in Paris will take different forms for a more direct link with the audiences, and not with journalists who serve as intermediaries. Thus, the press briefings of the Russian Ministry of Foreign Affairs, led by spokeswoman Maria Zakharova, are getting close to it - she uses, expressly and in a measured way, - the language of the *same* and makes jokes that are almost certain to become viral on Russian networks.

Opportunity 3: more videos!

For commercial brands, often the ultimate goal is to appear on television. This willingness is an anachronism, which is proven by the overwhelming majority of quantitative and qualitative analysis. Political brands are in a slightly different position, since the most established of them have privileged access to the "big screen". But, on the other hand, they lose a lot of competition on social networks to videos of cute cats and other animals. During campaigns, candidates' videos, often truncated for manipulative purposes, are distributed everywhere, but in times of "peace", reaching the attention of the desired audience with this excellent mean somehow falls of the agenda. However, video remains the most popular information format consumed online. Small extracts, often shot in GIF (animated image without sound), sometimes even replace emojis to become no more and no less than elements of language. Mastering video production and distribution is crucial knowledge. Again, many politicians claim to do it well, using *very* expensive agencies to do it, but the result is rarely achieved, if we compare the return

neopolitics

on investment of political videos with those shot for brands and their digital strategies.

Opportunity 4: more spontaneous and "real" connection with its audience

This is one of the direct consequences of this changing role of the intermediate bodies mentioned before. The removal of the exclusive nature of media "rendezvous points" for candidates (I repeat that the politicians in place are also the candidates, specifically those to the maintenance and support of their activities as elected or appointed) creates the opportunity for direct contact that would not seem inconsistent to society. Social media is constantly evolving and the availability of live broadcast options such as Facebook Live, Instagram Live, YouTube Live and many other ways allow brands and influential people to communicate with their audience in real time. Interestingly, it is the culture of video games that has brought to the notion of *streaming*, i.e. the live viewing of an event, this unique importance thanks to the *Twitch* service. Even if the politicization of this technology probably dates from late 2013-early 2014 and the Ukrainian revolution. At the time, the *streams of* protests on Maydan Square in Kiev played a major role in the conduct of the events, and the website created to ensure the uninterrupted availability of these images (*Hromadyanske*) then became one of the most influential young media in the country.

You don't have to be on all channels, but you should consider which channels make sense for your political brand. And if you're not tweeting live about your important events, you should really get started...

It is important to remember what we said in one of the previous chapters: "classic" media no longer impose the agenda: they now recover it from the social networks. Thus, even if politicians all over the world still like to maintain close relations with the classic media, it is sometimes necessary to wonder: is accessing the headlines of a major newspaper through its contact with the editorial staff is really better than doing so through the power of a post on Facebook, carried by tens of thousands of *reposts*?

These opportunities, integrated into the media strategy kit alongside the instructions duly developed for implementers, and reinforced by the message structure guaranteed by the Neopolitics Brand Map, make it possible to ensure greater consistency of one's presence in the media than that of competitors. Because this is one of the sad observations that can be made by analyzing in depth the "new media" landscape: despite the colossal sums spent on the services of spin-doctors, agencies and experts on all sides, the final performance is often mediocre. This is probably not due to the lack of skills of these agencies and experts, as they are often real professionals. Rather, it lies in the poor connection of media strategies with

neopolitics

the client's political practice. And, sometimes, in the poor training of the executors of the strategy. The gap thus created between perfectly designed plans, very well-defined brands and sharp tools and macabre reality, or any small crisis becomes almost a matter of state because its management is so catastrophic, is - and this is perhaps the worst consequence - taken up both by traditional media and digital communities (often heated by political competitors). And this recovery generates considerable damage, the volume of which is systematically higher than that of any measures that could be taken in advance.

These measures in response to the three challenges mentioned above, given the opportunities mentioned, include, for example:

1. Have content templates to publish in case of emergency on networks to save time needed to prepare a complete response. These models should not be aggressive, but rather have a positive agenda. They must be able to be set up in a few *minutes*. For example: someone posts on Facebook a video of a collaborator of the president beating up demonstrators during a protest action on the public highway. Of course, we can do nothing and hope that nothing serious will happen. But there is a risk that the "real" media will take care of the matter, that the outcry will appear on social networks etc... While a small message posted on the official accounts of the administration concerned, with an

image prepared in advance, and indicating that the necessary checks are underway, can otherwise calm the game, at least give arguments in the possible public debate: that we immediately reacted! As a result, this type of message must be ready for a wide range of potential crises.

2. Technical solutions (such as the discreet French application Azimuth5) must be used to monitor the "rising stars" of social networks. They must be contacted and used as opinion multipliers, but also as human intelligence to capture digital trends. But how many political administrations have services dedicated to relations with influencers? Putin's has one, but where else?

3. You have to manage your communication channels - Facebook pages, Twitter accounts, Discord communities etc. - in such a way that, if an opportunity to strike an opponent arises, a device provided for in the kit can quickly be set up, and the community activated.

neopolitics

Conclusion

As I said earlier, the precise solutions cannot be spread out in a thin book like this one. This is not because of their somewhat secret nature, but because to go further in defining the necessary policy tools, contextualization is mandatory. If only because every political brand is unique as it should be. And to communicate this brand to its target audience, the means, and the proportion of their use, must be consistent with the content of the Brand Map, failing which regrettable false steps of all kinds are almost guaranteed.

Context setting can be done, at least at its most basic level, without the participation of an external expert. It is just a matter of the decision-maker asking himself the questions in the following table:

	The neopolitical brand	Permanent competition	New media and the new speed of reaction
The big data	To what extent does my brand correspond to the expectations of my target audience?	What do I know about my target audience and those of my competitors?	How effective are my advertising and communication campaigns? How can I improve them?
The changing role of intermediate bodies	Is my brand close enough to the social reality? Has it been developed in a natural way	What are the relationships between my competitors and the intermediate bodies that	Do I use new media well to build a direct trust relationship with my target audience? Is my online

	from the real actions and convictions of myself / my party?	concern me? With my target audience? For my target audience, who are their opinion leaders and what are the structures to which they belong or are supposed to belong?	reputation management team responsive and professional?
The neotruth	What kind of defenses against fake news have I put in place to not let others discredit the elements of my brand? Have I done any stress tests of my brand?	Have I identified the sources of potential fake news attacks? Do I have offensive abilities with fake news against my opponents?	Can my resting capacity, my image management structure in new media, work at any given time? Have I trained my teams and myself in rapid and effective response to sudden and high-profile crises?

This table represents, in a way, the structure of the neopolitical layer of the external aspect of any political action. Answering these questions, which will be perfectly understandable to those who have read the reflections and observations contained in this short book, will be the first in diagnosing his or her political action - or that of someone else. As with the Neopolitical Brand Map, analysis can be done in any direction: you can (and should!) analyze yourself, your competitors, or your idols and models. Searching for vulnerabilities makes it possible to

neopolitics

exploit them, but also to eliminate them. Finding the breaches makes it possible to sink a ship, or to close them and keep it afloat.

There is no magic recipe. No incredible technique. No agency or political strategist can guarantee the outcome of a campaign, or the successful receipt of a reform.

How will the major changes - big data, the role of intermediate bodies and the new direct communication with sources of legitimacy, neotruth - be instrumentalized? Because that's what it's all about: taming these changes and, through the media strategy kit, using them as fuel for the powerful missile of the Neopolitical Brand Map.

The purpose of politics is, as Jordan Peterson would say, to reduce evil, to reduce suffering. Protecting those who are under our responsibility, giving citizens the freedom they need to achieve their potential for well-being: these are the necessary objectives, whatever the social model. But to reach the position of these responsibilities, and to remain there for the long term, we must constantly wage a fierce, merciless battle against the intelligent people who make good use of the often considerable resources at their disposal. The neopolitical nature of today's world also provides additional layers for this struggle. New tactics and strategies are not only desirable: they are necessary, unavoidable. I tried with this book to define the basics. In my work advising political actors, in my cultural projects - whether in the United States, Russia or

Morocco - I find new evidence every day of the changes I am talking about on these pages. And I believe that sharing these observations can inspire both specialists and general public to perhaps invent new instruments, to ask themselves new questions, to remember the important humility without which any social action is likely to be in vain.

In the same way, independent of any publishing house, I will continue to develop my theories and propose to the general public the tools I used to reserve for my clients. And I sincerely hope that they will be useful to at least some of my readers.

Printed in Poland
by Amazon Fulfillment
Poland Sp. z o.o., Wrocław

64149231R00087